BOOK OF DAYS

Phoebe Power's *Shrines of Upper Austria* (Carcanet, 2018) received the Forward Prize for Best First Collection and a Somerset Maugham Award. It was further shortlisted for the T.S. Eliot Prize and was a Poetry Book Society Recommendation. Phoebe's other publications include *Sea Change* (Guillemot Press, 2021, with Katrina Porteous), an illustrated pamphlet about the Durham coast; and *Harp Duet* (2016). She is currently based in York.

Book of Days

PHOEBE POWER

CARCANET POETRY

First published in Great Britain in 2022 by
Carcanet
Alliance House, 30 Cross Street
Manchester, M2 7AQ
www.carcanet.co.uk

A CIP catalogue record for this book is
available from the British Library.

ISBN 978 1 80017 178 7

Concept design by Andrew Latimer
Typesetting by Emily Benton Book Design
Printed in Great Britain by SRP Ltd, Exeter, Devon

The publisher acknowledges financial
assistance from Arts Council England.

CONTENTS

BOOK OF DAYS

for Elfrieda

Blessed are you pilgrim, when you contemplate the "Camino" and discover it is full of names and dawns.

Beatitudes of the Pilgrim

I had wanted to travel light, of course, but there were always certain things I could not throw away for either practical or sentimental reasons.

Matsuo Bashō, *The Narrow Road to the Deep North*, translated by Nobuyuki Yuasa

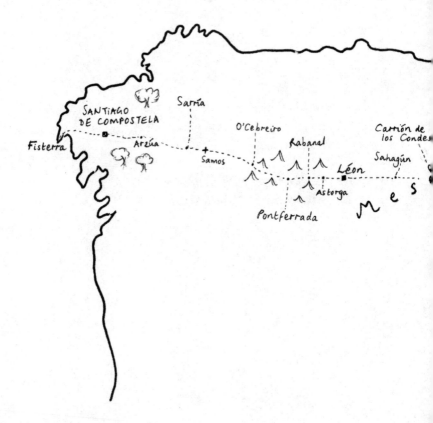

Orisson • St. Jean Pied de Port

Zubiri • Roncesvalles

Pamplona • + Zabaldika

+ Eunate

• Lorca

Torres
del Río
• Azqueta

Tosantos

a

Burgos

Grañon

• Logroño

Castrojeriz

San Juan
de Ortega

- Navarrette -

Frómista

Santo Domingo
de la Calzada

I walked up the slope on asphalt, feeling the road under my soles. I wore red sandals and a cotton dress I'd had for a few years, white with a print of bold red circles. It was the second week in June, and hot in East Anglia. I was in Ely, heading towards the cathedral at the centre of this subdued town, with its small high street.

That morning I'd woken up in my student room, unhooked the helmet from its peg and cycled to the station, where I found an available space in the rattling city of racks for my bike, and clipped the lock.

I saw the cathedral. I admired its front view, standing on the stretch of green outside. I could glimpse this leafiness from the inside, too, summer daylight framed by cool rectangles of stone. I processed down the nave, gazing at pillars which seemed weightless or pencil-drawn, hanging on nothing, and at the octagonal ceiling, holding up the roof and sides like a set of interlocked wrists, all golden-tipped and gay with green and purple.

At the back were some iron trestles supporting circular trays, on each of which were placed several burning candles. The flames were soft and mobile, like water. While the walls were old, the candles contained the prayers of the present moment, holding the touch of human hands, and recently made. I wondered what I was going to say to James, who'd agreed to meet me the following day. I knew what it was, what I was not sure I wanted to say.

As I was sitting on the bench on the station platform, ready to go back, I thought again of the candles, swimming in their pools. Could I be baptised? Just as I was thinking this, a nun came and sat down next to me on the bench. "You know, one of the Most Important Things in the faith is baptism." She was wearing huge glasses with plastic frames and a baggy T-shirt with a wooden cross swinging over it. She had a beaky nose and an assertive, butting-in kind of manner.

She spoke a lot of things to me, on the bench and afterwards, on the train. She had been born into Judaism but later became a Christian. She was first a guitarist and a singer, and on several occasions had tried to become a nun, but was not able to or had not been permitted, so had started her own religious order. You don't know what God has planned for you, she told me. If we knew everything that was going to happen in advance, then we wouldn't do anything, we'd be too afraid. Like me talking to you now!

She talked and I didn't have much of a chance to speak back, or rather I was tongue-tied on matters relating to 'God', let alone Jesus or the Church. Nevertheless, she gave me a gift as the train pulled in and we parted: a book. It was her memoir, and on that day I accepted it gratefully. On the inside cover she wrote my name,

> Who is also on a journey
> Shalom

I

I see through an open doorway a well-lit room with a long
table and at least twelve places set for dinner, soup bowls on
their plates.
   I bring myself in and appear
   definitely, in the centre of the room, new
   pack on my back and feet in boots immaculate.
   Excusez-moi, I begin bravely, 'xcusez

   Monique est lá. I am in luck. There has been a cancellation
and so there is one space left, one bed
   and one more space at the table. The others are now
   at Mass. Le dîner est à huit heures.
   Taking the layers of things from the bag, and into a plastic
sac
   to bring upstairs, the packs and boots are left
   outside; they are not mixed up.

   Bunkbeds vacant, except for one girl
   lying down with her phone. Emily. She is sick.
   They've been here three days now, it's like home, we like
this place, the food is good and they are so nice.
   Soon Michael comes in to see her. They are two students
just finished school
   and walked from Czechia. Do you not believe me?
   They've been camping, and stayed in many priests' houses.
My leg started to hurt and she is sick, so now
   we are resting here. We won't make it to Santiago, that's
OK, they'll come back. We thought we could fit it in three
months but we go to university in Prague in two weeks.

I sit at the end of the table by the open doorway, still summer light.

The Hungarian, Georges, has asked that we pray together before the meal so we

> do stand and hold hands
> and silence pour deux minutes
> and a man halfway

down the table speaks something strange, like a spell, and afterwards says that it's Jesus's prayer at the Last Supper, in Hebrew: he tells us this in English.

Monique asks me to translate what Sven says into French, for those at the other end.

Uh oui, I stumble, c'est la prière que Jésus a dit...

Georges' passport was stolen somewhere on the way from Budapest to Bordeaux.

> Tricky to sort out, actually it was a challenge
> set by God to test my resolve, to see was I ready.
> I have had many difficulties
> but a year ago Jesus called me. She called me.
> Stole my passport, all my money.
> I went to Paris the Embassy, Consulate,
> all these buildings they kept saying you have to wait
> a minimum of one week to get a passport.
> I said no, the Camino, I can't wait a week, she called me.
> The only way they gave me was a passport
> for émigrés, for les exils!
> Now I'm an exile from my own country, from Hungary!

2

There are pieces of bread to eat for breakfast dipped in
bowls of milk and coffee, dishes of orange and red jam.
  Sven comes down with his wife Cecilia: they ask for eggs.
He's a priest
    in the Church of Sweden and on his wrist
    is a black tattoo of a cross inside a circle.

On the road outside I see Clare from the airport, strapped
up ready to go.
  I am frightened of having to share, the first day, so tell her
I want to be
    alone. We creep separately
    around the church. The morning is twinkling white.

  Up the road, up it goes.

from St. Jean

      vending machine
      in shed.

      folds of mountains,
      folds of mist!

  I feel the phrase that God is good! Because the sun is on
me, I am an opening flower

    it gets hotter as I climb

      beautiful-shelled snails
      on the fenceposts!

At Orisson everyone's American, long-legged, crammed around with beers.

I'm just not used to this much bread, and when it comes to taping… we've read the books and we're just not 'doing' blisters.

Clare says, this isn't exactly peace and time to think.

What's your program, how many days? A date you've got to finish by?

By yourself? What, the whole thing?

At this moment, on the forum, in Chicago: when Spring comes I shall be buying myself a quality rain suit. I am wondering if there are any poncho fans out there who can tell me why I would want to buy one?

I had wanted to travel light, of course, but there were always certain things

> You should be slight
> to pass through the eye of a needle
> but this slimfit jacket cost £110

From the centre of the café I look at the flumes of the view, mountain-mist folds in every direction, and draw in soft pencil.

I would like to be doing a bit more of that kind of thing – sketching. A young American with neat edges, like a new toothbrush. I'm Matt.

He sits down beside me
but I want to be alone, and make excuses.

*

My mum is here with me. You can't see her, but she's here.

I am here to ask God what he would like me to do.

I don't know the reason yet, but I will.

I'm not happy in my job.

I'm here because my wife said it would be good for me.

I'm here to look after Noreen, my wife.

I'm here with my brother from South Africa.

I'm here to celebrate being able-bodied with my mom.

I'm carrying Dad's ashes.

I'm about to turn fifty.

I survived cancer.

We want to do this while we still can.

I've been working for the past six years for the internet, and I'm always on the internet, so I want a break from the internet.

I've just turned sixty, and I want to see what else life has to offer.

As you get older you realise what's important is people and I'm here to spend time with my buddy.

Lisa, Anna, Kate, Clare, Takla, Rachel, Gay, Cecilia, Sven, Jerry, Noreen, Laurie, Matt, Marta, Gurnell, Bo, and more

3

All set off together, start in the same grey promise.
Walking in one irregular string
    up the mountain, first one, then another further ahead,
then twos and threes, then another one,
    figures climbing with their packs of every colour: maroon,
turquoise, purple, yellow. Mostly we keep the silence,

from Orisson

        breathing up the hillside
        like a moving monastery.
        Cattle bells

    tung continually.
    At dawn the cattle settle by the side of path. Who comes
today?
    They take photos, carefully creep by or barge through,
transmit respect.
    The cattle let all pass.

    Clare peels off another way to swim in the view, alone,
resenting those who follow her. We watch from above

        and come to the Virgin, where the Norwegian
        ladies sing from hymnsheets
        among the rocks. Folk from the coach
        parked up take their picture. Frailer women
        with make-up and drawstring bags
        get out to photograph the statue's space
        but she looks outward, to guard the mountain;
        you cannot see her face.

Clare says
Mum's skirt's with me and I can feel she's around, when I
look at that view she's there.
  I've got déja vû right now of walking in the Lake District
down this walled lane, heather, ferns
and into a dappled wood – she
slips and falls! Gets out poles and herbal solution;
we are more careful

    beech leaves and quiet
    shadow spaces, sunny
    trunks of sky-grey lichen

till Roncesvalles, the abbey like a fortress.
Clare goes on to Burguete

      *

I sit in the vestibule, rolling my feet over a rubber ball.
A man walks by, sees me and smiles, speaking in Spanish.
He sits down beside me and grips my foot in his hand.
Takes it, actually, gently,
  in the crook of his knees, next to his thighs
  and massages it. My feet are very cold, from wet sandals I
wore in the shower.

    Más calor, he says
    rising to leave me there;
    más calor!

I drift into the abbey church,
and draw the carving of Mary holding Jesus.

It's very dark, unless you put the coin in to light up the
front.

A candelabra with a shell at its base: I draw the lines of
the shell.

Laurie says her son walked across the entire U.S. when he
was ten.

It was just something he always wanted to do. Now
he works for Apple. I don't know, when they hit eighteen
something changes; he doesn't speak like that to me anymore.
We were real close when he was a kid.

She's amazed when the main arrives, a whole trout with
eyes. I never saw it like that before.

During the Mass, some people stand up to photograph
the priest in his gold garb.

Five or six locals with feathery, balding heads and beads
keep us straight by singing the chants at the right time.

¿De dónde eres? one says to me, answering the smile
I want to give them.

4

Rained in the night, in shorts, cold knees.
Alone, then you hear

    steps behind or in
    front and know it's another
    you, boots in the leaves

down little paved tracks, and across streams.
Into a wider path and there are cows in it.   *from Roncesvalles*
Tranquilo, the herder says, and I try to be.

In the corner of a field I crouch to wee. At my ear a
beautiful web,
    dew-filled silk beads.
Up the farm track, hedges and grasses thick with the same

    hanging guardians
    on thistle brushes
    or across seed-heads

and after some time, half a walking-day gone and the sun
a golden burn now, we all recollect
    in this bar, rucksacks leant against chairs and I spot
    Laurie, Matt, Clare; Bo and Gurnell both from Norway –
    many queue in the noise for a cafe con leche or cut of
tortilla, hot from the plate
    while among them old men share fish lunches, relax and
play cards. It's Saturday.

Coming into Zubiri, there's Georges, yellow cap on backwards.
We hug. How is it? So hard, he replies, grinning widely.

Matt saw a guy walking, not really talking to anyone, in a really
quiet and monastic way. I admire that, he says.

*

Why have you come so far? Gurnell asks Jin-young from
Korea, to my left at the table.
Fire in her shy eyes, bites lip. It's kind of a
long story!
Tell us! We have time.

I was studying long time
and I didn't see my friends

twelve, fifteen hours a day
on computer, on my own

never saw my friends
I messaged them on phone but

I forgot how to talk to people.
So I quit my job

and come on this Camino
to talk, to meet the people.

There – it's hard for me in English
Thank you! We cheer and whistle

To Jin-young!
Thank goodness you are here!

5

We exit Zubiri separately, by the industrial park. Cats and
kittens

watch the people pass
from their ledge.

At the halfway bar Matt says he brought *The Idiot* by
Dostoyevsky. You're kind of nerdy, he realises about me. A
girl called Katie's brought her pocket Bible. Isn't the print too
small –

She's nineteen, with a soft clear face and more definite
calmness than any of us, like a stem of aloe.
I was thinking Zabaldika, I say; me too! Shall we walk
together?

Katie says, I've talked to God since I was ten years old.
I say, I can't find a community where I
fit. We stop on the path.
Do you mind if I pray for you, real quick?
Straight-backed, she's a silver pillar a head taller than me,
white sunshine lighting her face. She

grips my arm,
looks skyward, and speaks
directly to God.

When I think she's finished, she starts another
paragraph. Never falters

in her choice of words, articulate as levers
in a new machine.

When she's done, we hug;
I'm crying

At Zabaldika, Clare is resting in the garden.
A nun's arms gather us inside the church, and gives us a
paper to read as we float

Beatitudes
of the Pilgrim

around the nave.

Then we climb the tiny staircase to the belfry. The
floorboards ancient, hold us. All is a velvet silence. The two
bronze bells

hang in cut-out spaces
framed by air,
metal inside stone.

When we come down, Clare is gone.
The plan was to stay overnight but it's only 1pm and a
long afternoon stretches on with nothing but sun through
the leaves, sitting and talking the hours with Katie. I don't
know how much longer I can stay
without being absorbed into her, so I break myself off
onto the hot onward path.

I hope I don't regret it –
Whatever you do, she calls after me,
don't do that.

*

And one day I climb into the walled
interior, and the old town is less
yellow than expected, cardboard-grey
and buildings fold their shadows   *Pamplona*
down the sidestreets, where students
drink on pavements: last day
of fiesta, shreds of paper. A giant
puppetface waggles, striped
and looming, then in the next
bulge of the street a sudden bundle
of accordions. Hurry. Home.
Now I don't recognise a soul.

The hostel's a church made into a barn, a hundred stalls
encased in turquoise glass.

I tread the aisles along faces in their booths, listening for
English voices.

Irish laughter. I dare. Excuse me, can I eat with you
tonight?

The blonde woman beams of *course* take a seat come with
us – Deb? Ron? This is – she's going to come out with us. I'm
Ciara, this is Deb, Ron –

thank you for asking us, really how brave. Go and get
yourself something warm to wear.

Deb's in catering and orders the tapas: mushroom, rounds
of goat's cheese, mini hamburguesas. Everything's too salty,
rich but I eat it all

Ciara knocks back the gin in a big round glass.
She's planning a career shift, to pursue an
entrepreneurship idea, I know it sounds a little strange but
I want to set up a currency. Kind of a

Currency of Kindness, to motivate people
to be kind. I suppose it will be
a kind of an app.

The evening's the colour of meat and Ciara's dyed hair, in
contrast to the green and white of Zabaldika.
Thank you for letting us help you, she whispers, while Deb
and Ron draw cash from the machine.

6

The streets still grey with night. On my way out, past
coffee bars and shuttered veg shops, I pass a man begging
from pilgrims.

*from
Pamplona*

In my pack is some leftover bread from the tapas night in
a plastic bag. I trace the few steps back, and hand the packet
over.

The young guy behind sees me do this. Tienes grande
corazón, he tells me. Simone.

For a while we walk together, reaching for shared words:
I don't know Italian and his English is very poor; we try in
easy Spanish.

His bronze hair is scrawled up in a tail at the back; he has
an ornate tattoo manacled round his shin and a lovely face;
I'm embarrassed in my glasses and walking clothes. When we
get to Cizur Menor he vectors away

and I spot Matt across the road, in his helmet-shaped hat.
He's hurt his knee and limps a little, matching my slower
pace, so we climb together out of city, into landscape

suddenly cool and open.

A mountain
stands ahead, tall and dim,
prickling with wind turbines.

Matt's not happy in his job. He's been a work adviser,
teacher, restaurant server.

Now he's thirty-three – like Jesus
says our guidebook. Despite his knee he's walking faster
and after a while we separate

our different ways along the stream, unable to make
a commitment.

I stop with the expanding hillside,

    curls of olive-brown
    soft-ploughed soil, or mottled blonde
    picked out in lemon green.

What are the masses of stooped
sunflower heads, gathered black and brown
at their fizzing centres

and bowed in waves across the slope?
The crowds of heavy-necked souls, climbing
Purgatory mountain? Or us, just as we are,

    describing the sunflowers to each other –
    yes the seeds are pressed
    for sunflower oil

    Deb and Ron and Ciara ask me how I'm doing. Do I want
to share some lunch?   *Zariquiegui*
    I sit happy with a piece of tortilla beside Bo, sketching the
stones of the church from my plastic chair.

    And all the way to the crest, where silhouettes of cattle
and pilgrims prance in wind-clattering iron and through long
grass, ankle-deep, with nothing to absorb the rush:

Princes Gigantica,
Energia Hidroeléctrica
de Navarra.

Tread downhill and the rush of up disperses, hurrying into
soil and roots.

At Uterga, Matt comes by: do you have a minute? I think
we should maybe – exchange some information.
You mean like a number? But I'm not using my phone. I'm
sure we'll meet again.
He walks away. For the rest of the afternoon I sit in the
sun with Jin-young, drinking peach juice.

*

Takla's threading up her blisters. You know,
I'm beginning to think it's kind of like a river. I'm not in a
rush, but the current kind of pushes you along. It's like a tide.
We're in all these individual currents, at different speeds
that separate, re-join again.

Upstairs, Maggie and Aileen
pore over tomorrow's route,
complaining about gradients, hips;
I tell them I admire their tenacity, at their age.
We don't feel it, Maggie snaps,
bony as a stripped leaf.
They do up their lips and eyes
in blues and rouges;
go down to eat.

7

We're like beads on a string – here closely together, here
spread apart
    and it is still night. We praise the moon, which is full:
    looking back over hills we crossed yesterday, turbines at
our shoulders

    and follow the silvery thread of the farm-path, turning
yellow towards morning.
    Our bodies are bowls, scoured grey with waiting: a longing
for pictures, words, the shapes of churches, milk and coffee.

    The little church is delicate, her chin jutted upwards.
Golden stone *Eunate*
    filling up with sun. The inside's locked this early, but we
can walk

        around the octagon hedge surrounding
        cloisters built around
        the stiff-angled centre. Grey
        and honey, like the moon – west
        and east lights meeting – round
        and firm as a plate
        held in both small hands.

    We leave in search of breakfast, find it at Obanos, toast
and butter. It's still cold on the seats outside, TV playing in
the bar.
    Angelica's face opposite mine, fingers wrapped around her
coffee
    cup.

I list intentions, and proliferating
    gentleness
    gently and slow

    the opal shape
    of a treetop
    in a garden

the path we follow
marked through a car park;
arrows under our feet
flow through, thread between

and into cobbled elegance; it's opening time for shops
selling vegetables and pan and gratefully I present my
Spanish and warmth so far collected, and receive in return
smiles, interest, tomatoes, cheese.

On the way out, the bridge is
slender, it holds.

Puente la Reina

Little stones lodged together:
triangles and rectangles

irregular, no duplicates.
Like Eunate, feminine.

Step back to admire eyebrows
over el río Arga. Then

climb gravel again, in whitening sunshine. At Cirauqui some men are drinking in a bar. I thread past, through the stone archway.

Then a little later, stumbling over cobbles someone asks if I've seen the Roman road? Four prison officers from Dublin. Jack says,

this man in London, not bad at all and I could sit and drink with him and a good laugh but then on the subject of Brexit it wouldn't have mattered what I'd said.

But you've got to be grateful. Back in town we saw some kids in wheelchairs, give anything to be doing what we're doing, at least we've got our legs.

He buys me a bottle of water from a stand along the path, no it's yours.

They stop again at the next bar. Did Jack tell you we're all jailors. I sit on the plastic chair and take off my socks, stretch my feet.

How're your legs? Oh, she's lovely legs. I leave them drinking

*

She is also named Jin-young but older, more fluent and compact, light reflecting from her surfaces as she turns a Rubik's cube

Lorca

in the quiet airy room, alone. I'm not reading, she says,

I want to rest my eyes. See, I stayed an extra day to rest, this blister? On my pinkie toe! It's so nice here, and José is so kind.

I just bought this, to keep my mind awake. I want to see if I can do nothing the whole day.

I'm working on two things, the other is making my bag less. But I can't throw my hair conditioner!

I was walking with people and had some really good conversations, like girl stuff. I'd like a husband but all the guys in Korea, I go on dates but I don't really like the guys. They don't want a woman who likes to talk. I had a long talk with José about it, his wife's Korean, she lives here.

After that I've been walking by myself. Just pass and say 'hello' but keep walking.

My mother and aunts say I'm not really religious because I don't go in the church. They don't like that I live alone. But I'm forty now, I think I have to decide.

Isabel, who's walked through all the forests of Puy, understands that all Korean people are not shy!

Gyung-mi, with soft ginger dye can barely walk from pain and also wants a husband, preferably with an English accent. She shows me her exquisite baking Instagram and ASMR, Autonomous

Sensory Meridian Response videos on YouTube where the sounds of

e.g. strawberry chocolate

feeding a mouth makes you relax and comfortable, this is how she sleeps,

while next chair down the big Dutch guy

on 40k a day and can't stop, he's quiet

at dinner till adding to the marriage theme his wife is so much littler than him but he loves her, she's at home with the kids but he had to do this, walking so fast but he knows he's running from something

while Stu and Sam heaved their instrument cases mute on their backs until this night, when they bring out their strings in lightness, her mandolin and his guitar

to play in the open doorway, music all over the road, we

assemble in dirty clothes and sing or tap the wooden stools,
José too and others drawn from the hostel opposite, desiring
to be part

8

Jin-young stands outside in pink and grey boots, neat and
rested, her hair in two long plaits and round glasses back on.
    She holds up sticks, ready to go: I'm going to walk far
today, she says, I feel good.   *from Lorca*

The church has zigzags all around the arch: boys are
lounging on the steps.   *Estella*
    Hey, where you from? They're Dutch, with tan, taped-up
calves. Stopping here? No! We'll walk another 30, 35km.
But we haven't met any pretty girls along the way. You're the
prettiest girl we've met so far. But I am going in the church

    and the cloisters in the garden, tourists trapping them
with iPads:

        pine cone fan
        or netted fruit
        like a heart bunched-up –

I draw its
        three-pillar twist
        down the A-line

*

    The other Jin-young is just ahead, stumbling on her
blistered toes. At the wine fountain, Maggie sips from a
long-stemmed glass
    she brought from Sydney for this purpose.

Turn the bright metal tap and red bubbles out
like water. The two Jin-youngs
have found each other; I waver not far behind
Sven and Cecilia

The path gets high and sandier;
finally we talk. There was one of their children who died
very young. Cecilia was a nurse. I tell Sven
who is a priest, I need – but haven't found – a community
I can be myself in – and fear my family, others' judgement –
and everyone's opinion for whom the Church is –
Sven says, maybe
be bold. If you say with conviction, 'I am Christian' you
may find
– and I don't find a place there
where I fit. Keep thinking on it,
says Sven. One of our sons is your age. We want to take a
photograph, Cecilia says, to show him, to say we met you.

*

Thomas busies, opening drawers of sheets. He is telling
Takla: *Azqueta*
I guess I still don't know where I'm going, but I saw I had
to leave, about a year ago.
I was a victim of abuse as a child, long time ago but you
are always catching up with the thing. Running, or looking
for. Anyway
I was walking this time last year when I stopped here and
met Elena. She was managing the entire place by herself, so
I stayed and helped out a fortnight, doing odd jobs.
After I finished the walk I came back. I usually stay a few
months, long as the visa. I wash, cook, clear up;
actually I hate it

but you love Elena
yes

The Americans are lapping up the health food, houmous
and squash soup, aubergine stew. We talk of supplements,
online reviews and prior reservations, carbs and 'real' beds.

Look I got this message from Chris. He's already at Los
Arcos. He says the church at Los Arcos is AMAZING!

Then the masses of dishes, residue and clumps of rice
grain, multiply on surfaces. Nobody wants to clean.

Elena has gone out in the car to collect her daughter.
Thomas: I don't know why, she can walk, it's only 1.5km.

9

We wait an hour in the plaza till it's unlocked, then
pilgrims pour in, extensive gold vision of riches, rrretablo.

Seated in the centre
the little (black) virgin with blue eyes
from C13th and modelled
from the island of France
where they have a lot of black virgins.
In 1947 they *restored*   Los Arcos
her and *removed*
her black colour. Smooth black hair
and tight, smiling eyes,
her cheeks all powdered.

Meanwhile, painted faces scream
their letterbox mouths, cross-eyed
on the trompe-oeil organ

The retablo generally
cold, spiky: solidified
gold going to break off in bits

Every few metres,
stop to adjust the straps. Pick up.
    stop to drink. Go on.
        Sit down. Sven and Cecilia   *from Los Arcos*
coming through trees, don't see me.
Unlace, toe joints
click and stretch soft pink, dry

and hardening. Wrap
again in new soft socks; resume.

*

Jin-young and Jin-young arrived earlier on; now they're
cutting bread and tomato at a table set in the doorway.

I shower, bring my things and notebook down to be with
them. The younger, quieter in English, lets the other do the
talking:

Torres
del Río

We haven't found any young men on the Camino! They're
too fast; the women go behind with the old people

We're going to cook Korean food at the next albergue.
We'll find – what's the word? Sharekitchen. We're gonna
cook noodles. You can have with us!

I lead us to the tiny church, twinkling a few metres
from our seats.

swept-up arches,
faces in the corbels:

wind   ears
man   cat

      fish
        mouth

a tight arch-knot
roof, islamic star
and circle at its navel

and the chequer relief
outward, flickering squares.

The other girls have left. The site attendant
chatters in Spanish, louder than the building. There is no
consecration, no
permission to bathe here

*

At dinner I feel
sick and have to leave abruptly

blue, & orange, gold
& the gold coming down,
filling up the red   *from Torres del Río*
   leaves

and matching my geranium
shirt, ocean-
   blue shorts

   people still try
to take pictures of the sun,
clicking along with their sticks

…and I think about Stainton C. of E. Primary School, the hymn books that were so surprising to me, their soft covers printed in blue (Book 1) or green (Book 2), titles printed with a chalk effect and drawings of laughing children with bowl-cuts. They soon got a new, plainer set with glossy covers, and by the time I left the school we were singing along to CDs. When I was six I found it hard to read the words at the same time as singing them; I didn't know the tunes and I sang the word 'chorus'.

In assembly we put our palms together to pray and I watched the skin on my wrists wrinkle up in folds. We peeped as our headteacher Mr Shelton closed his eyes, and could not see us. We eyed him in his resolute quietness as he spoke on our behalf: we watched him in his weakness; he was at our mercy and hearing the grace the first time, Mrs Grant's abrasive FOR WHAT WE ARE ABOUT TO RECEIVE and the children bang their lunchboxes bawl MAY THE LORD MAKE US TRULY THANKFUL then pop their cheesy Wotsits. I didn't understand the incantation, its strange grammar and call and response. It was the same the first time I participated in Evensong and the psalms were sung with breaths in certain places according to the commas, and I didn't know the words of the creed or the confession which were not printed anywhere.

Recorded singing *Viana*
adds to the dead feel

    old retablos
    hanging off the walls

all the saints are strong
    white knights with polished heads

    virgin de nieva with a crisp silver head

*

John from Hull joins us for dinner: he's compact and muscular, doing it all in 14 days with a tent. *Logroño*

Why? we wonder. Well I'm a fit lad, and wanted more of a challenge.

Philip arrives sorry I've been at Mass. He works in Dublin with ex-offenders. Have you met the jailors? Ah! No, but I'd know them.

There's not enough room for everyone's plate, wine, water and bread: John's water tips over the paper placemat. I'm a born-again Christian, he's saying, faith, that's why I'm really doing it, I should have said that before.

He scrambles from the table, skipping dessert, and sets off in the dark again. He'll camp on the path, between towns, wherever he happens to land.

Well I couldn't do that, as a woman, says Caroline. I came because I wanted to prove to myself that I could, now that I'm sixty. My father used to take us in the car and just drive, he had that adventuring spirit. My mum still worries but I always had that spark of adventure in me.

Philip's plate of fish peers over the edge of the table and tips up on to the floor. No dinner for a hungry pilgrim? But the kitchen whips up another – flash-fried, Philip says, and it's fresher, more delicious than the first.

Somewhere out of town, we come to the crosses:

```
  t                      s                                     p                        s
 twigs                   t                          p         bits                      t
  i                      a                           r        c                         r
  g                      r                          flags     k                   anything
                         t                           y                                   p
                         e                           e
                         d                           r

    s a w n                                                        d
    t                                                              r
    r               b                                            wi s p
    i             t w i g                        z                 f
    p               t                            i                 t
                                                 g
                                                 z                        b
                          b i ke                 z                      b i  c
                          rusty              plastic                       c
                       c h a i n                 g                          p
                                                                            e
                                                                            n
                                                                            s
```

lifted in their chain link
    fence
            above the motorway

                    linear
                        shrine symbol of

                        keep trying

                    bending broken crooked caught

s   t   c
c   w   w in d   r
r ibbon   bits   m o re
a   g   s
p   s
                                                                        e
              t   c   s
              w   r
            sti ck   reuse   offcut
              g   a   h
                                    t   pi ece
    rope   l   e   n
    blue   e   t w ig
      a   n
      s   g
      t   st r i n g   h   knotted
      i   h   a   another
      c   l   n
                                        f   e

                                                    49

appears like an island. I climb to its hulk of honey-
coloured church.

    A cluster of girls in black and white spotted
    dresses and clicking heels
    fill the street for a minute and dancing

*

 I'm in the bathroom when I hear voices and the sound of a
door unlocking. I know straightaway it's

Clare! Who are the others?

Courtney and Emily, friends from Melbourne. I was so
happy to find them this morning, says Clare, going slowly
with an injured ankle since Logroño.

And we'd been walking mostly with men and had some
actually – bad encounters, says Courtney; we were saying
what we need now's a Girl Group, says Emily.

They change into flowered dresses; Clare puts on lipstick
to head to the bar; I've got nothing besides my grey, practical
outfit but go with them, overheating in the sunny afternoon.

The rest of us get beers but the girl called Rachel
has vodka orange juice. Hydration! she glitters. Tanned,
calm shoulders round her halterneck straps; she's tall, fluid,
hair pulled back and fringe.

And she can speak fluent Spanish – Gay, her mother
says – so she's been starting all these conversations, which is
lovely to see – I only wish I could participate more.

Later, we're eating veggie paella from low, flat pans and
drinking white Rioja on steps beside the honey church.

I ask Gay what she likes to do most, now she's retired
from the high school. Well, she glints kindly – I would have
to say

Building Community.

Meanwhile, Emily is telling Clare about the way some
men trigger her

Energy, says Clare, which is your gift. Look:

> lifting her fists
> fire eyes
> black sparks –

don't ignore it, says Clare. Use it. Sometimes I go to the
tree at the bottom of the field near my house, it's *my* tree.
And I just scream.

So we go to the top of the steps of Navarette; Rachel
knows the place, where there's a park like an observatory

> spinning the landscape
> round us, back the way we walked
> today and the way we will walk
> later, and the shoulder of the church
> beneath us where the town unfolds its boxes:
> supermarkets, banks, families and dancefloors;

> Clare stands on a slab of stone,
> high priestess, and we are six:
> Courtney, Emily, Gay, Rachel, me and Clare.
> Clare intones magisterially, her sentences
> clear as the prayer sends out in all

shooting directions

and when we touch hands, wire up our
screaming it foams away
in circles round us, Clare leading like she was born to do it,

    Kali, chest lifted high
    in wind and breastplate
    I love you   Mummy

to land and air, arms
banging drumsticks, jumping on coals

*

We take our dancing and jive like children at the night fiesta:
   the singer in local glory and chunky heels gathering in the
town and leading the conga line.
   Courtney and Em get another bottle and six glasses; Rachel's
the best dancer; she dances with Emil, a Dutch pilgrim. He can't
unglue from her upright ribcage, her smooth joins, her flicks.
She holds the wand

* * *

The next day's Sunday and Takla says
   there's a special Mass at one: they are going to swing the
botafumeiro.
   I wander in, among the women dressed in beads and blouses.
Normally I can't sit through it all but today the words I don't
understand lap me like a rock; I am still and think of N., a
person who hates me.
   I press him in a hug with all of the love I can to expel the
pieces of cut-up anger in him, accepting the flow of inevitable

words towards the breaking of the bread, and when that's
over

    the real excitement begins, tension is pulled
    into the ropes and it's going to
    lurch down and towards
    the heads of the people,
    rushing of emotion

        up, the joy of weight
        flying fast in a still space
        just because, because of joy

    everybody claps
    and the scent spreads everywhere

    Later I go back to the disc of green on top of town, where
yesterday we screamed.
    Others are already there, sitting on benches, to think –
    I think we're all the same –
    I left the Jin-youngs and found Clare and the girls;
    they left and I find Henny from Korea, in the kitchen;
    she gives me pieces of orange and I share my salad made
from a cucumber, avocado and green pepper.

    Certain conversations like when
    James saw Christ in his tent.

    I meet a nun on a train
    who gives me the book of her life.

    Sven says, think on it;

Katie: God wants us to –

last night I dreamed of him;
I want to see N. and

I am reminded I can also dance
with the others, at night, not always
an eye on a pillar, watching.

Adorning the body is to make of it a shrine, bringing spirit
out in form. No one would wear plain clothes to a wedding.
I see myself with torrents of blonde and multicoloured
hair, dressed in purple and flowers, covered in rings.

And also I cry.

*

Rachel and I spend the evening
watching a recital of Basque dancing.
Doughnut garlands
of paper flowers passed
gaily and overhead; castanets
and ribbons crossed, and handkerchiefs.
The littlest children
lean on the edge of the stage,
entranced: the swish
of the skirts and elaborate ease
of which patterns drawn by feet tie
and untie over and over, their mums
and sisters so skilled and smiling, hair
pulled back and bright
lips, the magical clicks.

13

Along the road in the dark with Rachel; we lose the signs;
we keep together.

   moon's a silver
     half penny

    plaster statue   *from Navarette*
of a saint and a pig
turning green in the dawn

Every hundred yards or so, Rachel
skips forwards, builds a cairn:

   small, site-specific
sculptures positioned

      stone
        by
      stone

    to leave a sign,
     to balance

Her shoes grip her toes to the ground in 'barefoot' soles.
Are those really comfortable? Perfect!
I once spent a while re-learning how to walk. How?
Online. You know Alexander Technique?

After 10k we reach Nájera. Clare is still in town with a
bad ankle, on her own in an Airbnb somewhere.
Rachel has the address, it's on the edge of the city, back
the way we came.
We have to retrace the arrows
to pick our way back to Clare.
No. I won't go. We're racing on a running stream
and I won't beat the current
back, slowed-up, repeat.
We sit at a cafe table in the plaza, our hands around cups
of té verde. Rachel looks into my eyes and says
When I was sick, my friends visited me. I know Clare can
look after herself, but I'm going to go back.
You're making me feel bad, I whine,
but anyway I go, go on.

The road to Azofra is baked and alone,
exposed, relentless.
Guilt circles on the river surface.
Know I have to swim again,
nonetheless, despite,
now we're here.

*

Azofra is one desiccated street. A pilgrim grocer's, crammed with split tomatoes, biscuits, flies; two bars; the hostel in a barn.

Booths divided by partitions made of uncovered chipboard, sawdust smell: hamster run. Each booth with two bunks each
and its own swing door. The blankets scratch.

I cross to the little shop, pick a banana and satsuma. A tall American man follows, watching what I buy:

Hey! Why didn't I think of that? and chooses the same items. I'm not in the mood to talk.

*

Later that evening I come in to find Rachel, eating rice and salad at a long table with four curly-haired Italians.

How's Clare? I ask. Oh, doing great. She made herself a big pot of chicken broth. I ended up staying much longer than I expected, we had this really long conversation…

14

When I wake up the clouds are pink but everyone has left;
I'm one of the last and setting out, the sunrise is long over.

That man from the shop is tailing me. I stop to drink and he
catches up, says Hey. Do you want some company? *from Azofra*
I say, no. He lopes further on; I see him speak with someone
else ahead

and walk to Cirueña. Rows of model houses, duplicates with
garage and white shutters stand empty, unopened. *Se Vende*:
glossy signs hang on each blank property. *Llame*
89574857633.
Behind the bars of the recreation area, the blue pool filters
itself.

At the motorway junction, a couple of buildings from the
original hamlet still stand:
Café Jakobeo. Through string beads, a woman and a few ham
rolls

I am like a loose pin
in the map of pathways,
shaken end-to-end or side-to-side

On the edge of town I spot Rachel with her Italians
outside a coffee shop, but they don't see me and I walk on, till
we cross again

in the church, and I show her the painted hen-house
set high in the wall like an organ.
From 1350, *a la catedral de la calzada,*   *Santo Domingo*
dónde hay un gallo y una gallina blancos.   *de la Calzada*
Behind the glass screen claws are rubbed in sawdust, heads
pecked, white feathers greened with excrement.
Standing below on the carpet, we cannot smell the smell
but know it's there. We watch their liveness like television

*

Arriving at Grañon by mid-afternoon, a queue up the
stone stairs
of the church tower. Soft brown mats laid closely together
in the eaves. There's a piano downstairs; someone is saying
I've written this song – is anyone musical?
Rachel's already there, adding syncopation and a showtune
cadence. They head out to the grass to practise; I follow.
Too warm in my woollen shirt, while Rachel in her
halterneck, her shoulders which glow, sings

and when I join we start to harmonise; it grows some jazz
hands, leg kicks in our tall, light sopranos.
The composer, Sam, is delighted; the others around us
watch. We record it on Sam's phone. Sometimes Rachel sings
the lower part, sometimes I do.

We gather round tables pushed together. Grey and slender Jan walked here from the Netherlands. He asks me the why question, and this time I say

because I wanted to.

This suits Jan. Right! No one does anything of his own free will. A wish is planted in him by an exhibition, a conversation… Because I wanted to, yes, a wise answer.

Sam says he's doing it for enjoyment, just that, I thought I'd enjoy it and I am.

He's a yoga teacher in Hong Kong, his eyes a bright brown-gold, his body a warm baton.

When Rachel moves off by herself to open her voice in the clear acoustics of the church, everybody follows:

all meshes, magnetic, energy falling off her in waves

*

The pilgrims make dinner together here – slicing onions, shredding garlic.

The one in charge is Mike, the same I snubbed this morning. He is managerial and considerate.

So many hands, almost no labour. I cut cucumbers and toss the salad.

Henny says, now I have your salad twice! First in Navarette, now here.

*

Jan is doing t'ai chi on the lawn

On the low wall, we sit listening
as one runs his hands on an electric guitar,
his hair long, face tired.

He is a beautiful guitarist, gentle
and exact, like brushing the tops of
individual blades of grass. The songs lap

into one another, not lifting his hands
between them. We stay,
pretending to write in notebooks, or
filming, to say we saw it later.

After dinner we collect in the church balcony, where he
plays Scarborough Fair, which reminds me of England, which
is his home also. I see its emerald greenness you can only see
when you are absent from it, in a yellow and dry land.
    Shep is about himself and his guitar, not God or the group,
but now a candle is passed
    around for each of us to speak. The Korean girl whose name
I do not know, with soft ginger hair and a strawberry face
    looks into the light of the candle and speaks with simplicity:

Thank you, God
And thank you, Jesus
Amen.

    *

But in the night, squeezed on my mat with others
like mountains sleeping round me
I wake up with itching

over my skin, like crawling
from the sleeping bag seams.
Can't move from where I am
resting in the crowd

15

I walk with Rachel, Sam, Jan and Tessa
into a pearly blue morning.

    combed stripes   *from Grañon*
    of fields and the sounds of roads

    yellow-brown stone
    churches, the colour of the haystubs

We twist figs from an overhanging tree; I ask Sam my
question.
    I do a group run every week in the park, I see the same
people. They're nothing like me but we chat, get a drink
together after.
    Then there's the gay community, and I have the yogis. So
it's not like one group, more like
    a tessellation –

I imagine the bees
zooming to Sam's
warm eyes, his smile.

Jan says, he and I are like brothers. We discovered that
he'd say something, and I'd be thinking exactly the same!
    We watch him ahead of us on longer legs, already
rounding the hill.
    But you have to part sometime. Him in Hong Kong, me
in the Netherlands.

You're a little bead
alone, and then
together, alone
and then together
zipped along the stream

to Tosantos

I cross the square in Belorado
to the cashpoint, encounter Gyung-mi,
hello, the Jin-youngs have gone on
to Tosantos, and Marie,
I don't recognise her large eyes
for a moment I met her in the bar
in Azofra

I am starting to forget
the order of the letters in place names
I am not the only one

*

A yellow house
with soft brown beams. Welcome,   *Tosantos*
a young man in bare feet
soundlessly opens the door.
This is an Hospital, not an albergue.

I fill in my details beside a man from Ireland on the short
settee, then Joel leads us up a set of wooden stairs, deeply
worn and shining.
      Mícheál unpacks his washbag. He's a large man with
shoulder-length, tangled hair, grey ox eyes and a soft mouth.

I wonder what you think about this, he chats to me. I've got a theory. The Irish are more spiritual than the British, aren't they? …

I go down and spread my stick of bread and packet of cheese, tomato on a table in the garden.

Someone else appears. A man like a skinny streak of brown-black paint, yellow teeth: Patrick. From Czechia, but he walked here from Finland.

Why? Because he's carrying Martin.

Martin died on 17.01.18: Patrick set off from Helsinki, a place loved by Martin. He set out in the winter and it was very hard.

When he got to the bridge between Sweden and Denmark they wouldn't let him cross, it's a car bridge. They found him in the traffic. Patrick explained, but the Camino, Santiago, to bring Martin. They respected it but wouldn't let him cross

…Then the bank in Amsterdam closed his account. He stopped his job in the restaurant to walk, so now, no more money. I telephoned them, why you do this?

In Holland he sold his cold gear he no longer needed; it was summer now.

Then he was robbed in France. At the cathedral in Le Puy, bags stacked at the sides and they stole his rucksack, tent, passport, money.

So now I have nothing! spits Patrick, lighting a cigarette and grinning through his cracked-up teeth.

Today I walk 57km to the donativo. It's too far. His leg is wrapped in a bandage up to the thigh. But I have to continue, to bring Martin to Finisterre.

He goes indoors and I'm still eating my lunch when a

contraption approaches. Some kind of bicycle festooned with panniers, a trailer full of luggage and a yellow flag on a pole, at the back.

Its rider walks towards me and holds out a palm.

Hazelnuts? But how to crack them? Oh, use a stone, he suggests. He roots out pliers from one of the panniers and drops them on the table, then goes off to park the bike.

I eat the nuts I can crack. Bits of shell stick to the kernels dryly, making them bitter to taste.

I'm joined on the bench by Marco, from Milan. He pulls out a tin of Italian cigars and offers one to the cyclist.

Whisky? He digs out a hipflask in return. The cyclist's name is Michael, Mick-aye-ell in three syllables, said the German way – but he prefers the English version.

No thanks, growls Marco.

After my first Camino, Michael says, three years ago – I didn't want to return to normal life and all those ass-holes I can't stand. So he took to his bike.

He's not travelling light. There are lots of necessary tools, whisky, bags of weed. This time he brought *Don Quixote*.

I leave the two men blowing rings, and turn into next door's garden.

A girl passes in front of the house. Her hair is a haze of springy gold, tied back; I think I have seen her before. I think she is French.

She sees me; our eyes pass around each other

*

We help prepare the dinner in the kitchen. I am cracking Michael's hazelnuts into the bin.

He stands with a stone and breaks them, while I pick off the shattered pieces with my fingernails.

Once he had a job as a landscape architect. He hates Germany, the whole system, all of them. Now he's free; no job, no house.

Rather than money, he likes exchanges. Once he did some gardening for a man, and lived like a king for a week. He bought towels and champagne!

Yeah, it can be lonely out there in the tent. But I'll keep on going, till I find my Queen of Hearts!

I go to lay the table in the chilly dining room.

What I've been thinking about today, Mícheál from Ireland says, is orange.

Orange? He's a painter, he tells me. I'm getting this from the landscape we walked through. I've been seeing the female body in the landscape.

Oh, ok, right.

All artists want to paint the female form, he says.

The Franciscan monk whose house this is, sits at the head of the table in a green tracksuit.

We eat salad with pears, and a rich red stew of potato, onion and chorizo. He brings us seconds, third helpings – as much as we can eat.

I'm sitting next to Mícheál, who leans in close and predicts I'll have a child soon.

Having a daughter was the best thing that happened to him. Amelia.

She's an artist too, he says. She has my hands.

The monk instructs us not to leave tomorrow before 7.30. If we walk in the dark, we'll meet the Devil.

At the top of the sleeping mat,
Michael's pink fluffy unicorn
mascot waits cross-legged
in place of a pillow.

16

Jan dips his bread in the jam and tells me his views on free will: we don't have any.

Our desire begins in the stomach... for instance, we say we want to learn an instrument, but we never start. Why are we walking here? Because a cord

pulls us along from the navel.

Jan likes Spinoza, John Coltrane and raga: at home he's got a big sound system.

He walked from his front door

down all the familiar roads, to Belgium

then along the woodland paths

of France. Now he WhatsApps photos to his wife in the Netherlands. She sends one back of a soufflé on the stove, creamy and yellow.

Trying to draw me home, he smiles, lean and white

-bearded, scoured

frame of a prophet or patriarch,

bright blue eyes.

gold lighting the
brown haysticks

clutches of black   *from Tosantos*
berries, thistles
and burgundy gorse

your walk rises
to meet the church in every town

At the café, someone asks if I'm good. Of course, says Jan,
she's intelligent and beautiful so that's good.

The wanderers
unhitched from structure, and all alone
in the landmass, in the forest.

Are they wise men
or fools? Are they Jaques?
What do they know?

    fewer women wander

autumn smells, pushing   *to Villafranca*
leaves, luminous red rosehips

the sunflowers drop their
heads and scatter
brown seeds, paper-dry

I fill up beside Gyung-mi at the water-tap; she offers me a
biscuit

If you need to do this,
the body says,   *to San Juan*
be patient with me   *de Ortega*
and I will heal.

A pink-faced man with white hair settles himself on the
tree stump, beaming at the music from the sound system,
trays of water and snacks in the middle of the forest.   *David*

This – is – fantastic! he declares, to no one in particular.

Thank you, we echo from our shoulders silently, turned in
another direction. His smile comes into us!

Someone taps my shoulder. Can we walk together for a
while? It's Mícheál again, the Irish painter.

I got depressed with the people around me at home, he
says. There's this woman next door – and she got married,
and she's not like, really attractive if you know what I mean.
She might have thought it was her only chance. And they're
sitting there every day, and they don't love each other!

I came here before and did the Camino in 33 days, the
stages. But I hardly noticed where I was.

This time I feel affirmed – not so much by the people, but
by nature. It's still here for us.

The Trinity according to Mícheál: 1) *Gaia* – Earth; 2)
Good Hearts – and many of them are here; 3) *The Way*, the
arrows, air, all around, directing us.

Can I tell you something? This morning, all I could think
of was sex. Then the most amazing thing happened. The
landscape gave me a huge kundalini orgasm

right through all of my chakras!

I was born a shaman. You're born one, like you're born an
artist. You're going to have a baby soon, like I said yesterday. I

feel it. But – maybe it means something else.

He shows me a picture of the cob-house he's going to build in Ireland.

I'll come and help you build it, I say. Mícheál and Michael with pliers, garden twine and hazelnuts, good with their hands and hazardous to women, lonely.

When we reach San Juan I want to stay; it seems restful.

    Still and white, nothing
    but bread and prayer.

Mícheál goes on towards Burgos

The priest repeats   *San Juan de Ortega*
   silencio
the peregrinación is about silencio

*

I sit outside, to draw the church in last light.
People cross in front to snap a pic.
But drawing is length of looking,
no photograph. By drawing I remember it
in its movement, the sun
whose colour from gold towards red-
pink coming out of rioja mortar
and the suspension of bells
in their arches. The bronze bells
hanging with their crosses
like tongues between the stone

17

Hilary's in the bunk above mine, her feet a mess of blisters.

We're the last to leave in the morning, stumbling through forest. She's a full-time mom with her youngest about to go to college, so what will she do now? She came for answers, and was assaulted by fears

> two beautiful old
> oak trees, a pair as if
> married   *from San Juan*
>   canopies
> blurred together, over
> the pink dawn valley

The cold sends us indoors for black tea and something to eat for breakfast. The girl is there
   with the haze of gold hair, tied back. She tells us she got ill a few days ago, and slept for twenty-two hours with a fever.

Her body had to get sick; now she feels lighter. Her voice is wondering and generous, like the edge of a wave over sand.

Anne-Lise and I walk on together. She explains that her mood's been up and down, like a teenager; sometimes she prefers to walk by herself but then she misses people, thinks maybe they don't like me –

yes, I say, I know.
The sometimes-alone,
     sometimes-together;
sometimes two and sometimes many,
     sometimes three or four
and sometimes alone,
          the lurch and throw of it.

There is a turning with no arrow. While we waver, a guy
catches up to us:
     he's Eivaros; now we are three. I saw you last night, he
says, drawing the church.

Together we climb a sandy hillpath, in phase; stop to share
some melon on a café table. As the heat of the day comes in
Anne-Lise and I change into shorts.

Set off again but Eivaros has seen another Lithuanian he
has to talk with; he'll see us later and the triangle is broken,
reverts to two.

We have to decide if we're going all the way to Burgos
today; we decide that we are.
     We look for the softer, green path marked on the map but
arrows push us on to grey, aching asphalt and it's turning very
hot.

Anne-Lise says she lived in Prague for eight years,
she is a musician

and afterwards went to the Balkans
with a guy from Macedonia.
They played in the bars every night, in love

with the folk music, special strange harmonies
but it was tempestuous,
in their apartment they argued

and it couldn't go on. She left him
but he followed, wouldn't let it go   *to Burgos*

It's long into the city, down the dry tongue of the highway.
We cling to the edge while buses and lorries heave past
their loads at speed, in mockery: this is no place for feet.
There's no one else of our kind in sight. We are an
anachronism, village-folk; our legs and uncovered faces feel
suddenly too exposed, viewed from vehicle windows.

Yes, she always wanted to be a singer. She sang at the
bottom of her parents' garden
    in Normandy, with a pine-cone, anything
    for a microphone. She feels when she sings she is giving
them something they are not quite able to express in their
lives,
    and they know this now, they understand that music
    is how she connects deeply with people.

She goes quiet as we make the last eight, then five km.
We're at our limits, when suddenly the town changes
    from billboards, torn shopfronts, clotted traffic
    to miniature cobbled streets. There is Tessa, Gyung-mi –
without packs at café tables, sipping drinks.
    We are like another species, arrived out of caves and
bushes, covered in dust. Anne-Lise can't stop to stand or talk

*

Walking again over the hostel's rubber floor, even to the toilet, after the day's km are done and we are already here seems unlikely, a miracle

and yet it is necessary to go to the cathedral. Soon I am passing out and in of the twenty-one chapels, an audio-guide to my head.
I try to calculate how long I can look before fainting from fatigue, take in none of the information on the boards, the art styles, dates, just walk
in a field of colour and paint and space

Mike gestures me over for dinner at their table in the plaza: I gratefully accept.
I love looking over at the evening

    tower patterned with nobbly dots
    like a harlequin coat

and talk with Stefanie: she came for two weeks and this is where she finishes.
Overall it's been a disappointment. It was harder than she'd thought and she'd had to send her bag ahead, etc. and this caused anxiety, not the freed-up feelings she'd expected.
I think you have to do it with plenty of time and no schedule, she says. On Monday she returns to Kölln, her job designing kitchen fittings.

On the way back to the hostel I come across my friend Eivaros. We give each other huge smiles. Hey – how are you! Good night!

18

On the way out of Burgos trees and birds have long been
up, folding and unfolding wind, while the people are still
inside, it's Saturday, asleep or starting to make coffee.
The city leaves me with the feeling I've missed something,
some monument?
All the exquisite paintings and buildings, plaster blocks
sleeping in dust

*

We're walking through a village called Tarjados. Someone
interrupts my silence: a bearded guy, Alex, from Basque
country. He only started out this morning; he's walking a
week from Burgos to Léon.
After our brief exchange he says, OK, I go faster, maybe
see you later, and launches off ahead.

We leave the village on a firm white track. The path
continues but I haven't seen an arrow for a while.
Up ahead are others: two Koreans, a Japanese man, the
Basque guy Alex; it's OK.

We arrive at a fork and still no arrow. There wasn't a place
to turn. Where is the village we should have come to by now?

Alex asks a passing local if we're going the right way to
Hornillos. She speaks at length and gestures over the hill to
our left.
She says keep going, it goes to Hornillos, says Alex.
But that's not the Camino, I say.
Yes, look, fine. Alex takes out his phone with map and

GPS. You can see that it's right.

I don't have a GPS, I say.

I could turn around and go back along the road, to Tardajos and find the real camino. But we've already walked too far, and the arrows have hidden themselves: they only work in one direction.

from Hornillos

I trust him.

We set off on a steep upward path. It's faint and sandy, like the line made by a rubber on the end of a pencil.

The village gets more distant, the space around us higher and quieter.

I don't really believe that the grey line on Alex's screen relates to this thin path we're walking on.

He's only got a sliver of battery left, an orange-red flash, 18%.

You're really worried, aren't you? he jokes while I try to calm my breathing.

He gets me to talk in Spanish, which makes me concentrate and laugh a little

The path flattens to a windy plateau. Grey grass, emptiness.

The shoulders of the other hillsides sit back round us: rigid bone structures, houseless.

Alex suggests we stop for a rest among some stunted bushes. I sit cross-legged and drink, while he stands and lights a cigarette.

It's ok, it's only 1pm, says Alex, if we walk six more hours we'll still have daylight!

The Japanese man goes by, his GPS lit in front; it's all right. Not long after, we see the delicious thing:
a blue sign with the yellow shell symbol, bursting with shining rays.

We are back in the midst of the thoroughfare
running like a broderer's thread
through desert, a deep-water channel carrying
people, speech, days on the move.

We were only off-map for two hours, like we took a scenic variation. The others who were never lost, tramp past.

Hornillos swims luxuriantly at the base of the hill, and Alex describes the huge plate of macaroni he's going to have.
The bond between us starts to soften. I say I'll buy him a beer when we get there, sorry for being a wuss.
He asks how long I've been walking; I tell him. He says, there's a Basque word for what you are.
JABATA: strong woman!

He tells me the name Hornillos means 'little bread ovens'.
It's one close, quiet street. The stones in the walls are rounded and cream-coloured, like little loaves.
After the plateau, the existence of Hornillos feels impossible, like a fairy dream or figure drawn in wind.

*

Right at the end of the single street, before you fall into nothingness, there is a restaurant in Hornillos. It provides the things the pilgrims want these days: vegan mains, bottled beer, yoga.
I eat some chilli there with Cory and Charlotte. Cory is

beautiful: his face shaped like an ocean, Pacific hair pulled
back with a coloured band.

Charlotte, his wife, says people along the way have
confused her with me, because we both wear glasses.

Cory has his laptop open on the table and a camera with
its own microphone attachment, a fluffy bunny's paw.

You brought your laptop?

It's light, he says, watching the room
through the camera's fold-out mini-screen.

loosed back
into landscape.

It's freezing and windy. There are two local women, their
heads wrapped in scarves.
Then I realise it's Courtney and Emily; they didn't bring
jackets

Blue   Gold

                                                        from Homillos

Land   Sky

The ridge is tall at our side, and covered in patterns.

At Hontanas we stop for fried eggs and Rachel
materialises; says she walked in the dark for three hours

At Castrojeriz I enter the Church of the Apple, with its

round red window. The door is open; it will close at 14.00.

I don't know the time. The man at the desk taps the DONATIVO box.

I tell him I want to look first, then decide.

No, no, he insists. Un euro.

¡Pero no es donativo! I slip the coin into the slot, and start to look around at the exhibits. The church is a museum now.

There is a a statue of St. James on his horse, rearing up to trample a Moor, whose head is severed. Santiago *Matamoros*: St. James, Moorslayer. Saint Iago.

IAGO

my pilgrimage

being done , as I am a Christian

in the circumstance of glorious war – my purse

Full of crusadoes;   I have

boarded

covered

topped – white steed

snorting

the   savage   Moor , poor Barbary.

Othello

Kill   i'th' dark?

I have a sword of Spain,
and put it home;

I took by th' throat.

We must obey the time.

The man is calling out and jabbing at his wristwatch. I don't know the time. I've only just walked in; I haven't seen anything, but it's clear I'll have to leave.

Pero un euro, I remind him. He's back behind the desk.
Quiero un euro.
He throws it down. Gracias.

I fall out of the church into sunshine, crying. Courtney and Emily are passing; they scoop me up.
I am confused; I hate the town

*

I've been bitten by now and try to wash
and dry things in the machine;
I do it together with Courtney and Em. We lie on our beds.
Emily eats a bag of chips, Courtney gummy sweets.

*

Yoshi plays his quena flute while Iuri and Angélica salsa between crowded tables. They're sexy, can't hold back their smiles and hips, shoulders exact; we sing enthralled to their wave till after the first verse
enough now, laughter into their chests and blushing; they sit again for the rest of the meal

Climbing the mountain, with a hundred others.

    path rises up brown
    its forehead.

turbines twirling, indicate
we are walking into the future –

    cold mornings, que frío
    and bright, hot afternoons   *from Castrojeriz*

at the top we settle, look around
and down and around

Imagine the return: not able to describe this
except in clichés:

    'I am full of love
    and light, Jesus and the star-glass'

Rachel is a healer, wrapping Angélica's arm in the
hermitage. Sometimes spaces open like parachutes, asking
can we sit and suspend

but the impelling force, forward arrow
sends us on like an addiction

    back to the open
    table. Four humps
    in field corners   *to Boadilla*
    like limpet shells

    or an arrangement
    of cuboid stacks;
    neat-bound hay the only
    3D construct on the grid.

    The only sound my feet
    on the tilled topsoil,
    my shell's clink
    on the clip of my bag

Rachel and I think we'll stop in Boadilla. Puppies and
cats nose in the garden; a small pool's layered with algae;
sculptures peeling.

I'm resting on clean sheets in the attic space. Anne-Lise
comes in, her hair golden, jacket violet / jade.
Another girl with red hair, resting two beds down. They   *Mélany*
chat: both are French. I seem to be asleep.

Jan is doing t'ai chi on the grass, and mentions the
hermitage:

I wondered if I'd stay the night? But it seems the will was not strong enough.

Rachel and me get a beer with two guys from Hackney Wick: James and Ed. It's a holiday, right? They're just walking a week as a break from their city jobs.

They say they support Labour and I ask if they find it hard, personally, to reconcile Left policies with the corporations they work for, e.g. shooting ad campaigns for Mars.

I don't explain my question very well. His eyes go cold, clammy, balls of grey. I recognise this –

> Mrs S (I am eleven) brings me into the library at
> playtime,
> > spits down my throat. *You know why you're here...*

> N., like a cold hard cat
> rips the pages from my book.

I am reminded of all that exists before, after, apart from and all around this delicate path, or 'fairy world', as Rachel calls it.

The depth of the morning, of all the days in which I have been gathering

does not change this. Yes, we will have to go back.

Talking to Brits and already it's all about class. James assumes I'm from a certain background; some tic clings on from his past.

Now I've got a bull on my hands. I'm treading water, wishing I hadn't come over here at all, looking for the pool-side –

Rachel's there, silvery cool: If I could just come in here.
I think what she's trying to say is similar to what I've
sometimes asked my friends who work for big banks.

Her tall preparedness
converts them into puppies
sniffing and bobbing at her every word

I scurry to Anne-Lise
spooning jam on her bread,
her calm. Loyalty of friendship:
whatever you did,
it wasn't your fault

*

Like a stone dropped   *San Martin,*
in water, it turns deep   *Frómista*
wheat colour, both
cool and warm inside.

Animals claw to capitals
in discreet places,
lions hang on to rims and
     men hang on with
          their hands on to
               the lions.
A lion holds on to their clothes with his teeth.

Some way in front, two figures: a large blue bag; a flume of
light-coloured hair.
     It's Mélany and Anne-Lise, speaking fast in French and I

can't keep up, tugging on their bag straps.

Both live abroad, spent years running from France yet they agree,

the people they've connected with most on the way are French. You can't reject your country, your language.

After a while I fall back with Anne-Lise, since we both prefer to walk more slowly.

The route slips on to the highway in full sun, the track dead-straight with waymarks every few metres, upright like tombstones.

Anne-Lise is just ahead. We keep silent, our heads tilted down to avoid the light.

At Villálcazar we sit on a wall and share chocolate and almonds. She will carry on – to Carrión; we laugh.

I linger and climb to the Templar church, its sheer walls like a prison or fort. I buy an orange juice and drink it gazing at the

  rose window
  like a dozen keys

around an eye. When I leave town it's still watching, guardian or judge.

The last part of the road I am silent, dreaming.
Are they waymarks or pilgrims
up ahead, there:
dark upright stone
or a person
moving? The tip of the spire

creeps up beneath – it grows
with your moving feet
if you can persevere.
Pilgrim, are you walking back
-wards or forwards
you are so far ahead

I lose Anne-Lise. We meet in the square, then look for
different hostels. I go to the other end of town but the
building's all shut up, then I can't find my way back.

Matthew, an Aussie pilgrim in vest and flip-flops, on his
way to the shop finds me and shows me back to his hostel.

The tall door from the back-street entrance clicks
and swings:

there are Mélany and Rachel, a polished floor, frilly beds,
maps and posters; it used to be a school.

They are bagging up Mélany's stuff to put in the sun and
fry the bedbugs. Her cheeks and arms are all puffed up from
the bites, Rachel's too.

Until yesterday I was walking with people who made me
feel suffocated, Mélany says; this is my body's reaction to its
boundaries being breached. We fill our rucksacks with a toxic
spray

then go and see the nuns.

By the bar on the way are Sven and Cecilia, who I haven't
seen in days: they're leaving today but will return next year to
finish it, God willing.

And how are you? Well, my sister is joining me for a few
days at León.

Oh lovely, Cecilia says, you can share the experience with

her.

Sven clasps my shoulder and holds my eyes. But now we have to go.

Everyone's crowded in the hallway, tucked along benches, crouched up stairs or on the floor.

On chairs at the front are three nuns dressed in beige. They are young and beautiful, clean white cloths tied firmly round their foreheads. One is playing a guitar.

They ask us each to tell about our reasons:

Georges is first and he breaks down, his wallet stolen then he collapsed in the Pyrenees, they helped him...

Courtney follows, weeping; then Melissa, Jan, David, Mélany, Rachel, me, Emily, Angélica, Henny, Vladimir and more

and all of us find we're unfolding
the inexplicable
crumbling round us in this space

and none of it is masquerade
and all of it is truth
and no one is scared to say
and all of us are safe here

While the room disintegrates in shapes of tears and broken sentences, the things we want to say,
the faces of the nuns stay dry.
They listen to each story
like the silver sides of stones

drawing in and reflecting the tide back
gently. After each has taken
her or his turn, one takes the hand of Georges
and speaks to him about it privately.

I'm sitting in the Mass beside Mélany. She points out a St.
Michael statue.

Again! she exclaims. He's my Guardian Angel. Every time
I meet someone on the way who helped me, he was called
Michael or Miguel.

You are light, the nuns say
You are made of light

You are not alone

They press stars into our palms

We hurry back to the school-hostel. Nicolas has prepared
dinner to share with us, Rachel and two Mexicans, Luis and
Francisco.

I wash Nico's cooking knives. He has made spare ribs and
garlicky pasta with chorizo; it's very good.

Our conversation darts between Spanish, English, French:
Rachel is annoyed she doesn't get the French.

Merci Nico. Avec plaisir, he replies.

He likes efficient organisation, economy and fairness.
After the meal he has me spoon the extra eggy pasta into six
plastic doggy bags.

Like a parade or glittering
conveyor belt, tread lightly,

it will take us there,
there are many of us

behind in front around
this train that's in

the middle of its journey,
not powering fast nor halting

slow but simply going   *from Carrión*
at some midpoint

we don't remember
where we started from,

Rachel and Mélany and I
drift into Anne-Lise

with a girl called Blandine
we gather in threes and twos

that plait then untie
alone, one spinning at the edge

we're leaves on the road
that the wind gathers up

then brushes apart again,
we're reeds with air

around each individually
but also a fan

breathing down the road
the way that clouds move

across a sky

Mélany moved from France to Mexico City where she
was a finance executive at L'Oréal
    but left her job and an eight-year-old marriage, and her
husband's little boy: she was like his mum.
    She had everything: partner, house, car, dream job, but
when she was hospitalised the second time, something had to
change.
    She'd lost the new child that had been in her womb, her
abdomen a web of pain.
    Her guardian angel appeared and told her she had to stop
– if you go on like this Mélany, you will die.
    She had not been honest with herself, and the pain in her
body was its response and a message.

We let the magnet pull us further. It gets hot again, we

unpeel layers, the wind licks our legs.

Once Rachel was on a freefalling plane. Not a joke: the cabin filled up with smoke. Actually nobody screamed; everyone just went silent.

Now I'm not a yogi or anything, but I was going all right, in for four, and out for eight.

And next to me was this most amazing dad
with two kids, who were crying and asking questions but he just said

It's okay. This kind of thing happens *all the time*. The pilot's just getting it fixed for us.

I wanted to say to this dad next to me
would it be okay if I held your hand?

I would just black out in that situation, I say. Me too, says Anne-Lise.

Rachel says, did I tell you about the time I was attacked by wild dogs?

*

Emily's feeling sick. She and Courtney report that Cory and Charlotte strode on ahead, 30k a day to reach the next vegan restaurant, but the Meseta stalled them. They think it was the water. Cory vomited the entire night.

Terradillos de los Templarios

I suspected bad water at first, but realised that pilgrims who drank only mineral water had also been affected [...]
It is only towards the end that you appreciate how tough the Meseta actually is, it burns you up without your realising it

Emily speaks quietly about it to Takla, who's a family doctor back home in Seattle.

Grouped on stools around the table, sipping wine instead of water. Our cheeks look red and mad.

Where have we walked from? We no longer remember the names of towns.

Only that we are here, our bodies tumbling over themselves

While Anne-Lise sings and plays guitar
Mélany swings her head in love;
the barman looks up while his hand
turns a cloth around a glass.
Behind the song, her fine-spun threads

the TV weather map shows
floods everywhere in Spain
except – it looks as if – on our strip;
we carry on in drizzle
down the lanes.

from Terradillos

at Moratinos, bodegas:
hobbit holes for wine
storage, snug in turf.

woollen quilts
wrapped around trunks.

Rachel's in the café already, on a stool beside the
condensation-covered windows.
Help me eat this fruit salad, she says: a deep bowl of

yoghurt, oats, kiwi, apple.

First Mélany and Anne-Lise join us, then Emily and Courtney drip in, in wide-sleeved plastic ponchos.

Now the rain is coming down steadily. Maybe we should just stay here. It's 10am.

One of my favourite things to do, says Anne-Lise, is just sit in a café with friends and talk, play music and drink tea all day.

I am close and threading
and unthreading with the other girls as we pass through a clearing, by another hermitage.

Courtney makes jewellery, her earrings swinging
silver all the way to Compostela.

I recently joined the Lapidary Society in Melbourne, which is kind of funny, all these old people who love stones, but the caves and minerals are fascinating actually. I'm taking pictures along the way of shapes I see like leaves and plants, to make maybe into designs later on.

*

At Sahagún, I go and find the architecture:

hollowed-out   *Tirso ruinas*
corinthian, empty
basilica.

tiny brickwork
crowds the curve
of mihrab or apse.   *Santa Cruz monasterio*

floor paved
with polished stone:
six-pointed star.

I search for the Mudéjar church. A face shines at a
restaurant window: Rachel, with the other two. Hey! Come
for lunch!
Wait! I'll loop back down. I just want to look at this first.
Beside the supermarket:

zigzag curves
pushed out in brick,
in series!

chorus of browns,
many rectangles.   *San Lorenzo*
tower suspended

on its arches
empty of bells.
birds roost

A couple of pensioner shoppers perceive me sceptically,
admiring the ribs of that old construction, dust-barn.

I climb back down: the others have already ordered. We
want the same: thick pizza with lots of vegetables.
Then a square of creamy white cheesecake with a heart cut
into it, and four spoons. Spanish cheesecake is grainy and not
so sweet.
Anne-Lise laughs and says she likes her men big in bed;
Mélany's ex in Mexico was short but she loved him.

I sit amazed
at this table, with this crystal,
the four of us,
willing it not to break or float away

Mélany has a list from Nico: we are to collect the
ingredients for dinner and divide them between us, to bring
to the next albergue.

The colours and lights of the shop are startling. We buy
leeks, rice, red pepper and chorizo.

The food adds a lot to the weight on our backs, but when
each carries something we'll share later, it binds us. Leeks
poke out of my bag's side-pockets like team batons.   *to Bercianos*

It takes us hours, we dawdle, teach each other songs and
pose for girlband selfies, vegetables growing out of our packs.

We tumble to the village and Mélany says
Look! It's Nicolas with his kite
in the next field, Nico, Nico!!
but he doesn't hear her

and we arrive arm-in-arm still singing
at some late hour, some U.S. volunteers receive us
and we are too loud and bonded; they say
like teachers, maybe it's time to calm down.
There isn't a kitchen here after all.

Rachel doesn't come in to the prayer but stays strumming
guitar in the next room.

The volunteer tries to 'bring the energy down' by playing
'Ave Maria' but it's tinny through her phone and we can still
hear Rachel's soprano fluting through the thin wall.

Behind the volunteer's seat is an ugly, salmon-pink Jesus
mural. She begs us to pray for her daughter, whose marriage

in the States is breaking down. I ask what it's like to go
home.

She says her old life leapt down her throat; she forgot
what had happened.

A Romanian man crumples, saying he doesn't know how
he'll face returning to all the 'rules'.

No, I say firmly,
wrapped in the day's light cloak
holding my crystal – we must insist
on bringing it back with us.

Right, says Anne-Lise, now we have a star
to take and show the others,
and help them find the same.
Mélany is quiet.

We are resolute, though unknowing
if we will succeed at this.
We are still children here –
arriving, not yet grown
up.

She takes the plate outside
to the village street.

    sharing my bacon
    fat with
    Calcetines the cat

I forget to pay and have to turn back

The way today is a slender line   *from Bercianos*
of green between the poplar trees
and the road, which is smooth
fast and dry.

A message from Patrick, in red marker-pen
on a large stone under a cross
among photos and pebbles:

    MARTIN
    10 - 9 - 1984
    17 - 1 - 2018

Nico's side-pockets are stuffed with kite strings, poles, his
cooking knives. We walk beside each other on the narrow
path.

He tells me about his martial arts club in Pau. It doesn't
matter your natural skill, he says. What's important is
discipline.

Men, women, children in my club: when it's like that, for
everyone, that's a good club.

We pass a picnic area, where Rachel's
balancing her hips on the feet of João: she is teaching him
acro-yoga. He's lying with his legs at ninety degrees, soles
face-up.   *to Mansilla*

You step on to shoulders, bones, air; you hold yourself
lightly.

Support in tender places, like the wrists, ankles, base of the
feet.

Nico's begun to fly his kite in the meadow. He lets me
try it, tells me to tug for left and right but not too hard, tiny
movements.

Twenty metres off he throws the frame
and the wind gathers up its gift, it shudders
up like a bullet or rocket then hangs
for a moment, tail dangling
before panic-diving back to earth,
brittle hay-stubs.

Try again: same thing. And a few more times. Once
it whirls, spinning manically like a Catherine wheel, and
swoops a bit.

Nico gives another demonstration, and little blue
dances with her arms out, freely
relaxing in the space.

When it's my turn again it casts up fast
then flumps back down, hurting its nose.
This could take a long time, I say. Practice, says Nico.

I leave him flying in the farmer's field:
he's a boy he's forty
cerf volant

*

The hostel is greasy and crowded, blocks around a
courtyard.
    A British man with pale knees is hysterical at Reception:
if I can just pull the mattress out to the floor that'd be fine.
Knee problems. I walked 43k today, I don't know I just kept
walking, anything to eat I'm sorry.   *Julian*
    The woman at the desk smiles beneficently; the staff just
got back from family lunch and siesta.
    I offer him a banana. It's only his first few days; he started
at Burgos. After weeks on the road, by now the rest of us are
like calm pitchers of water.

    Anne-Lise is washing her hair; it's a long process; she
plans it for days. Mélany cooks a pan of rice in the shared
kitchen, with the vegetables we bought yesterday.
    Many at the long table: Mélany, Anne-Lise, Rachel and
me; Luis, Francisco, Nico, Blandine, João. The cobs of corn
Nico picked from the fields to boil are not good to eat.
    We are very hungry; there is enough. The table is speaking
French, Spanish, English and Portuguese.

Then we turn our chairs ninety degrees to massage the shoulders of the one in front, a giggly conga. I am rubbing Anne-Lise gently, her delicate warm neck. It musn't be too hard, or intimate.

This is Mansilla; tomorrow, León
and I will see my sister.

The pilgrim in front has stopped
on the bridge to enjoy the sky.
I give him room.

gold and pink
        over Mansilla's
crenellations.

For those who are watching
remember we can do this every day

Jan and David ordered eggs and are sitting outside,
discussing Spinoza. I want to know more about David who is
so happy, with deep red cheeks.

When people know you're a priest does that alter the way
they approach you? Is it a secret here?

I am one of those people. I want to ask about the Church
in Britain, a community, me, how do I. I want him to grant
me something.

It's not a secret, he says.

We mount the hill overlooking the city.

How old are you, Jan?
Not as old as some.

People at home much younger than you would never imagine that they could accomplish this.

They're fixated on certain ideas of old and disabled, get to a certain age.

Do you feel anything?
No, I'm fine. But we still have some way to go.

Rachel and I scoot down the hill in zigzags.

I open my mouth to ask David. But I don't ask him. I open my mouth. But I don't.

*

The boy in front of us in the queue smells like a cowshed. A German woman tells him to wash his clothes.

He grins back. No really, she says. He looks seventeen. He and his friend walked from Prague with one T-shirt.

Rachel leaves the queue; she's going to go dancing (she's going to find João).

The bunkbeds are metal and crowded together and my bunk's in the middle, right beneath the ceiling light.

Rucksacks are stacked by the wall; smartphones crowd the power outlets.

I go out in the heat to wait for her. I wear my sandals and just take the guidebook and some water. We're going to meet at the Gaudí house.

The bricks are pale like tiles, the windows spindly. Jan is sitting on the bench opposite, eating quinoa out of a plastic container from the supermarket.

Good, healthy and cheap, he says.

I get up from the bench so we don't miss each other. Then my sister is there, wearing her glasses and bum-bag in neon colours.

Her idea of what she was doing – pool refresher, quick dip, lemonade and deckchair – was at odds with mine, what I was doing – still deep someplace, deep workings, still unfinished. Cajoled to the surface, fussed over and interviewed – that was bound to frustrate me and I should evade it, staying in my zone. Or, in trying to pull her under to join me at mud-level – she was bound to kick against it.

She: needing to stay at surface-level and within sight of her babies, floating in neon armbands round the islands. Me: sticking down deep, on the sea-bed, where properties were altering my composition in fundamental ways – a process I was well engaged in, must not now be interrupted – and for which I had paid dearly, snipping ties and swimming off by myself. Only this way can you reach the deep places, where the root-stems are pale and fleshy; only here are the most tensile patterns visible.

Trying to keep hold of those fibres while stretching out a hand to her was all but impossible. Bringing her down, she felt like she was drowning, lost and unguided in this dim-lit underplace. The sandy path, which reliably and safely wound down here, if only you could keep to it, was not familiar to her; she had not arrived by the path, but by sudden dive and submersion. And her, trying to reach with the ends of her fingers to me, while keeping buoyed enough to wave across the water to the small ones – wasn't feasible either. She daren't reach me, and even this far from them was too far. She lost their photograph. She put herself out – to where? And where did she want to go?

THE GREEN HOUSE

So I ran back to the others
at the Green House.

*   *   *

Anne-Lise and Mélany – sprawled among the cushions
and the tarot cards, bound up in greeting, like the puppies
downstairs in the garage. You're here!

Caitlin, with princess waves of yellow hair is at the desk.
Can I get you some tea? Camomile, sage? Her voice is a
little withheld, half-awake.
You can wash your cup or leave it, she says, someone will
take care... there's no curfew here, no check-out time, no
meat allowed. Yoga around seven, if you like.

You'll find you can't leave! a girl called Cara grins. I've
been here three days now and I can't get up to walk again!
And the food here is so good.

*

The yoga room is a warm, blank square.
At some point the teacher arrives: Viktor, wolf-like and
inexpressive. He leads the class to a slow rhythm, without
humour.

Imagine a miniature version of yourself. You are standing
on your tongue.
Then you jump, down the trapdoor black of your throat.
You are in the stomach cavity, full of bright, shimmering

colours.

Here, you are transformed. You are the self you wish to be.

We lie in Shivasana on the seabed. Our body cracks in
fragments.

As we breathe in, the fragments break off and drift apart
in the currents above us.

Breathing out, they settle back and reconstruct our body,
in an arrangement
different to before.

*

The food is bright and abundant, made from the
vegetables they grow here; cauliflower, pumpkin, beetroot;
bowls of wholemeal bread and salad leaves.

After weeks of mostly white bread, eggs and cheese, we
eat with our eyes and tongues together, the orange and green
flames.

The aim is to unify mind, body and spirit, Viktor says. And
the easiest way to do this is to walk.

I'll wander till I find the Queen of Hearts, said Michael, at
Tosantos.

Viktor gazes, tattoos glowing in the overhead light, as
Anne-Lise sings and plays.

He covets. What has been brought here, what element
of gold or precious medicine, what healing herb, and can he
pick and eat it?

* * *

We spend the day suspended, stretched like cats around the house and on the lawn.

The puppies have long snouts and silky, tan-brown fur; they lie back in our arms, like babies in their cradles.

I first met Simone a hundred days ago, in Pamplona. Now I hardly recognise him: his body seems to occupy more space, the particles that make him up

somehow drifted apart. His hair is looser, opened out in a wave and fanning his shoulders, striped with a coloured band; his expression softer and more distant.

Rachel can't resist this and they are in the garden, making shapes with their bodies under her tutelage.

Elegant, and erotic: the lit zones carefully stepped over and hands placed between, like observing the rests in music.

Twenty-two-year-old Simone can hardly hold the feeling in himself in the warm sun as she burns over him, dancer or bird.

Anne-Lise is not around. I sit with Mélany on the cushions and tell her about my sister.

It may have been too much to arrive suddenly, dropped in like this, we agree. She had to leave her children for these few days, her son nine months and daughter turning four.

Do you want children?

Yes! says Mélany, but I need to find the right man first.

She describes her dream of making a healing house like this, but for women. I have three women in Mexico who can help me, she says – but I'm not sure yet exactly how I will do it.

* * *

We don't leave early. Anne-Lise especially, finds it hard to
leave. I don't know where she is. My sister left a day ago.
The rest of us set off in patches.

stones on the path
like stars falling up from the body's seabed

and back in a different
arrangement.

make a drawing from this,
a shape, an arrow

29

Where are the working mums on this Camino?
That's right, they can't just   *from Astorga*
I know you think I don't have a clue but believe me I'm
less messed up than these people.
    I've got my marriage, house and family. That's what they
want too; they can't admit it
    You are selfish. Going off on your own, doing what…
'Spiritual process'. Get a grip. It's just a walk.

    Now it's just a walk, two blisters make themselves known.
    One near the ball of my left foot; the other on the inside
edge of my right heel, long and curved, like a puffy scimitar.
    I slap on the Compeed, blister cushion, too late and the
right one pops and tears as I walk. More plasters, and now an
ever-present soreness,
    fronts of my toes crushed against the boot-ends.
Something irrevocable is happening to my feet, the muscles
realigning,
    minute bones straining and working, holding together for
now, respect us,
    striving to mend, straining and working.

    Rain sits low in the sky but it barely comes, squeezed-out
drops on my face and hands.
    It's early afternoon but the light is grey and dimmed. The
path feels emptied out, like everyone's ahead.

I'm going to stop at the British hostel. The village is all
pretty stone and thinness; we have entered the sharpened,
mountain phase.   *Rabanal*

Knock and I'm in the Home Counties, telling Fiona what
I studied at university. My voice in English, to an older
British person, feels unpractised.

Fiona paces the stairs and there are pears in the orchard,
a fire in the grate.

I haven't asked, but imagine her stable with horses, two
grown-up children and plum trees, *The Times* on the kitchen
table, a village church for which she volunteers at summer
stalls.

She makes tea in an industrial steel kettle and the other
volunteer, Ray trails behind her, dispensing advice.

Something you must do, is go to Finistairia. His Cockney
vowels wring the word.

At Finistairia, you look into the sea, and you see into your
future.

Darcy has taken a book from the shelf, 'Returning from
Camino' and sits by the fire, quietly making notes. We need
all the help and advice we can get.

*

Caitlin from the Green House is at the row of bathroom
sinks. She left there the same day as us.

Now they need more volunteers. But I needed to leave,
she says, combing fingers through her pale hair. I only stayed
'cause I was sick. It got weird, the owner – but I still left
pretty late so had to walk in the dark over some of those
fields. I don't like that.

What's wrong with the owner?

He didn't want us to leave. I think he tries to get all the female pilgrims to stay and work for him.

What do you do back home in the States?

I'm a nurse. She plaits up her hair. That seems real far away right now.

30

Cruz de Ferro – highest point, arch-cairn – holds too
much expectation.
    When it comes it's a heap of our trash,
    left behind not brought with us.
    Stones painted with names and chemical colours,
    wrappers, plasticised ribbon.

    purple flower-heads   *from Rabanal*
    mark the pilgrim path like fingernails,
    like stars.

Two lost kittens follow the parade of school-children
along the side of the mountain.
They pick them up. Don't come with us!

I sit in the heather and slate
my cheese slices spread on stone,
    getting colder.
Gaze into outspread space and depth,
    the bird-silence
feeling elsewhere. Knowing I must eat.

A woman says hello. I don't recognise. She says, you
remember, we had dinner all that time ago, Azofra was it?
    Marie? I say. No, Kathy.

I have to stop to change the plasters. All OK? someone asks.

Yes, my feet pale and cold in bare air. The downhill gravel buckles our knees and hips.

A big bare tree   *to Molinaseca*
with a stag's arms.

Crunchy ball shells,
shiny conkers inside

like horse chestnuts, but these are different, related –

furry on the outside,
softer smash open

'self-indulgence'   'it's just a walk'

By the asphalt,   *into Pontferrada*
a man picking grapes
in his front garden
into a bucket. *Mira*. Meet
in the zebra crossing, presently
a car – holds
out a bunch of new grapes
damp and sweet –
we shake hands, quickly turn.

Pontferrada has a wonderful castle, locked with its
thousand pieces of different-sized stone.
   I buy a piece of almond cake in a white-lit cafe and sit and
eat it with Sherrie Lynn.
   When we enter cafés like these we feel a bit dirty, like
stems picked from the garden, covered in sun.
   Sherrie says she'll stay and visit the castle. But I can't
retain the information,
      palaces and temples like pictures on a gyroscope
      fluttering too fast for our slow bones

Will you go to Finisterre? I ask Bek. John says, Ah! That's the thing with human nature, first 'are you going to Santiago', then when we're almost there the question changes, are you going to the next one, are you going to Finisterre?

seed-heads blow
over my tired body
in the red and the leaves

Courtney and Emily, waving from the bar with glasses of red wine. They booked a lovely place just 1 or 2k further, do I want to join?

*

Anne-Lise: you probably noticed at the Green House I was flying!   *Pieros*

I stayed up late to play guitar and Viktor and I kissed.

He wanted me to stay, I was going to volunteer there but at the last minute I said no.

I thought, I have to go on, I don't want to lose sight of my purpose.

He keeps Facebook-messaging me, asking me when am I going to come back.

Viktor? Pah! Emily snorts. We wanted to get out of there.

I liked the way he did the yoga, but did you see the tattoo he's got on his foot? "Eat Pussy Not Meat".

After dinner we talk about love.

There's this singer I'm in love with, says Rachel.

I've never seen her face across the table look this soft, like wet sand.

She and I are friends but we live in different towns.

Rachel and Anne-Lise pass the guitar back and forth between them.

In the morning Anne-Lise is singing again.

Doesn't it sometimes get annoying, Rachel whispers, when she plays the whole time?

32

Hummocks of gold and red earth, purple and dark green cloaking the shapes of hills. We walk together in a band and talk a bit. It's a soft morning.

At Villafranca we're watching the stones in the castle walls as the sun moves over them, from dimness to sharpening, back to a blurring haze.

The walk from town is a lift up
by the shoulders,
on to the mountain level
and suddenly quiet.

Rachel said she'd walk with me on this section, but she's off ahead like a deer

her head bobbing, always 200, 300 metres in front
till she bends to build a cairn, takes some seconds
and I catch her a little
then she's off again, and the distance grows.

rosy conkers
springing out of spiny shells

crickets bounce
like springs! when they land
observe pink
their wings

traffic below
here a leaf falls
    two

Mountain bee
thank you for letting me watch
you suck the nectar from the purple flower

here's a praying mantis
seated centrally
like a guide.

The path winds up
through the portal
back in human territory.

Pimientos drying in the yard
where Rachel waits beneath an awning.

Anne-Lise comes panting through, her skin red.
Didn't bring enough water –

then Courtney follows through the passage, strong and
silver.

A huuuuge praying mantis landed on my chest, I was like
woaaah
    I saw him too! I say, I think it's St. James

Courtney and I shuffle back down the hill to the base of the valley.

The Aussie owner Susi opens her garage and Emily, Charlotte and Cory are there already, drinking tea in matching mouse-grey pants and tops, like patients or inmates.

We are handed our own bundle: QANTAS airline pyjamas with the kangaroo logo. The clean cotton, after weeks of the same sports' fibres on our skin, is delicious. It's the bedbugs. Some of us are wracked with bites, but we don't know where they are or who's carrying them in their stuff.   *Trabadelo*

All the smudgy scraps we've been wearing – underwear, socks, pouches for toothpaste or money, anything with a weft or seam to lurk or lay eggs in gets chucked in the black liners, to fumigate with insecticide then burn off in the sun.

I think they'll find us again in the next place anyway. Cory finds the thought of them in his clothes – or worse, hatching in his bag back home to launch into the carpet – too upsetting, you can't guard against them completely, and begins to cry.

But you're vegan? It's dog eat dog, he says.

*

In the morning when I retrieve my clothes from the liner they've lost their smell, flesh-familiarity from our four weeks' walk together. The fabric feels rough, impregnate with irritants, wicking into skin.

33

A series of linear settlements, with tiny bars and petrol
stations. Last of all and prettiest, Herrerías, where the horses
start from. I pass an empty stable yard, strands of hay
  and hanging lead-rope. A tree turned white

  covered in paper
  dreams folded
  up or made into scrolls.

Up the steep way, darkened by trees. The man ahead is
jamming to jazz trumpets out of his phone.

  Halfway up, a woman at a café table with a glass of juice
smiles at me.
  Lovely, isn't it? Always someone new to talk to. I've met so
many people.
  She tells me about her bad marriage. Pia. Drinks, cheated
on me twice, lied for a long time.
  I have to leave but it's hard you know, 37 years, a whole
life, children.
  When it happens I don't know what he will do. Does he
know what's coming?
  He's waiting in Denmark. But the Camino gives me
courage I didn't have before. When I sit on the side of the
mountain and look out I feel stronger, and glad again to be
alive.

The horses come rocking downhill the opposite way from
hoof to hoof, over uneven ground.
   This, their everyday task; they are wonderful to us;
   they are heading home for hay; we're on our way to
elsewhere.

   At the top we're clasped in a dewy cool; the stone colour
changes, turning more blue-white and ice-like.
   This is O'Cebreiro, sky-top – Galicia now, a Celtic land;
octopus with smiling mouths are painted on the walls. The
coast and its filmy airs
   suddenly nearer.

   Behind the racks of postcards, a very old church. Inside it's
cleaned-up and cared-for, refurbished sparsely, unpeopled

   but for a sweep of red candles:
   flames in their red glass pots
   spread across the floor and up the walls

*

   At Liñares I cook for Cory, Emily and Charlotte
   on the induction hob: pasta, onions, garlic, tomato, olives
and tinned mushrooms.
   This hostel's brand new, like a glass box.

   After dinner I step outside
   to where the shaggy cattle
   are tearing at the hay next door.

      The moon is nearly full again –

Someone leads a group of cream-coloured
cows and their bells go by.
Then they give their colour to the sky
as the mountains purple and darken.

A dog shouts his way through;
a person shouts to the dog.
The cattle next to me
stop their eating and begin to bellow.

The traffic sound, insects,
blackberries. All the voices of the pilgrim people:
Australian, American

Night falls; the people keep their lights on.

    Don't forget
    to look at the moon

Praised be the creatures
I love that the words of the Canticle
may be said and read many times and meaning
again and again and differently

34

red blood light

a grey and white church
   steps up to the belfry   *Hospital de la*
   open for birds or someone   *Condesa*
   else to sit in, or hide.

   Above the doorway, crowded
   lines in stone point down:
   enter here.

*

   rinsing down through the farms, wind clatters
                             leaves in the yards
     I enter like a dream walker

   ushered down lanes, processions of cows with their dogs,
jump
     loud energy barks, while cattle hold back their tune
     to their creamy hides
                & we pin back, part of the hedge.

   smells of manure and bonfires
     & a whipping, rootless rhythm down

     I love among the moulded sweeps
  of landscape, the hopeful rows of vegetables.
     Good green cabbages

squared-out on a hillside
                    or pumpkins & squashes
rolling around the garden, behind the house.

The sides of the lanes layered with hedge and root-wall
      metres up, and us dropped deep
in the crease, with keyhole
      oak leaves shining outlines overhead,
                    curly-edged

800-year chestnut

      nooks, handholds   *to Triacastela*
      ready to touch

      Rachel and Jake
      sit in the tree

      energy travels
      through the moss

35

Over centuries of running feet, trotters, people, paws: the
routes made snug into the land, metres deep.
　Walls stiff with roots, their canopies chestnuts, oaks.
Scurrying escape routes
　or passages into prayer, leading towards or away from
monasteries and farms. We're getting to a place of some
importance, footchannels quickening there from every
barrow and underhill

　and the monastery's resplendent, spread over a riverside,
only　　　　　　　　　　　　　　　　　　　　　　　　*Samos*
　the wall's so high and grey we can't see the trellises and
fountains or hear their singing voices; it is a kind of prison
　except there's someone in the orchard, filling the sacks
with apples.

　I round the top and the lens dilates: four or five
　　　enormous pigs　　　　　　　　　　　　　*from Samos*

　At the base of the slope a small stone hut, and in its apse-
shaped alcove
　the tiniest of shrines:

　　plastic Mary
　　standing on a cork
　　fanned by seashell.

No choir but one
bird.

*

I'm with Courtney when we pass a place with hammocks
and deckchairs in the garden, by the highway, just outside the
town.

Why not? It's up to you, she says. If you feel like some time
to yourself?

San Mamed del Camino

On the shelf of travellers' abandoned reads, I find a book
with a clean white cover, the spine unbent.

Sentences turn on their hinges; paragraphs open and
close their windows; in a deft second the brush is dipped, a
character made.

The story is set in a Suffolk coastal town in the 1950s and
it's the best book I've ever read. I haven't read a book for five
weeks.

The setting delights me, bringing a damp, ridiculous
England: letters sent by post, milk in bottles, profit in a book
business, helpful Sea Scouts.

I feed on the web of multiplying signs, old-familiar nouns
    suddenly bright. I steal the book, and keep it carefully
among
        my poems and prayers
        like a high energy
        food source, keep nibbling.

36

In the night I travel somewhere very deep into the paths.
    Courtney says she's been having more vivid dreams lately,
of riding out with the woods behind her.

    Getting close now and the streets are crammed with
mannequins clutching wooden staves in their armpits with
dangling mini-gourds, beside the racks of yellow arrow
magnets.   *Sarría*

    There's a lovely sculpture on the side of the church, of a
man with large soft hands.
    No-one knows who it is:

        Christ Pantocrator, David,
        Melchizedek? Craftsman,
        farmer, benign king?

    Keep passing down the string, through scattered
settlements but none have nameplates, so the map becomes
approximate – we could be here, or here.

        When I was weak and tired
        sitting on a wall
        un homme gentil
        de Bretagne m'a donné
        a beautiful biscuit
        inlaid with almonds

sweeter than any
  jewel

The eucalyptus leaves are long and slippery underfoot.
Courtney: feels like home!

Each path becomes the next and we've never arrived; it's
the end of the day and feels like we're already walking the km
saved up for the next, pushing it.

We giggle, air-light with exhaustion.

Courtney's lit up, tramping ahead –   *to San Xulian*

She always gets like this at the end of the day, says Emily.

Courtney feels she could get a stress fracture, how have we
not got one yet, how have we walked this far.

Rumours of a group of obsessive pilgrims trying to do
100k in a day

or a girl who didn't know how to stop, she was a medical
student, who walked all night and collapsed on the road.

*

Cory says Anne-Lise was singing in the dormitory again
and the people that were there said they saw angels enter the
room.

Rachel rolls her eyes and turns to me. For you, would you
say there's something spiritual in this experience?

In the end it's all consumption. We get up every day and
eat, buy more, spend but we aren't contributing anything. It
can't go on for ever. We have to go back to work.

PLEASE HELP I HAVE
WALKED HERE FROM ENG-
LAND WITH NO MONEY
NOW I AM TRAPPED.   *from Melide*
FOOD OR MONEY PLEASE.
WE ARE IN 2 TENTS WITH
2 DOGS BY THE RIVER.

Next to this, on a smaller sign: BE CREATIVE with a pad
of lined A4 and a tin of sodden poster paints. Rain and a
few coins in an upturned shell, beside offerings of browning
bananas and half-full bags of raisins.

Whatever you have you must be ready to share, so the
pilgrim splits his bread and medical supplies with his
companions, all along the way.

But something's unexplained. Who has walked this far,
1800km, to stop with 55 to go?

Is it a test? Some drop a euro or fifty cents. Others pass
and despise, disbelieve, keeping their money for themselves.

I don't have the courage or interest or sympathy to go and
find the tents, the 2 dogs, and ask. I am content to crouch by
this tree, transcribing their sign in secret.

Why do I watch and repeat, without responding?

Because their sadhu's wandering smells like pride, like pot,
not lotus flowers?

Because I am not like Christ, who gave anyway.

*

I cross another soaked pilgrim in the pouring, pitch-black
street.

I'm going to have a pizza here, I say.

We share an Xtra-Large between us. He's Nicholas, blond, Danish, about thirty; it's like a blind date.

Three weeks ago he quit his job at the software company. He'd get up at 06.00 and start his emails, carry on at work and later do the same at home.

He exceeds his targets, gets promotions; he's competitive he says, successful. Except he found there was no time left to enjoy life.

Arzúa

He went on holiday to Bali and Thailand but never with a girlfriend: relationships never worked out. And he had to admit that he liked his own bathroom.

So I've got three days left to figure it out, he says.

Maybe you need a hobby?

Oh yes, I do already, I work out at the gym two or three times a week, he says.

39

My teeth were breaking apart from my gums and coming out in handfuls and I had to go for an emergency appointment with Mrs Anderton, the dentist I had when I was a child. She had red hair and thin features, a gentle Scottish voice.

I had the dream where your teeth fall out, I tell the others. That means you're anxious, Charlotte says, or a change is coming.

I meet Cara again in the woods. She's solid and short with very white skin and long dark hair scraped back from her face.

She tells me she went to a girls' school in Hertfordshire: her accent is middle-class, cut-glass. As you would expect the other girls did History, Geography or Spanish at St. Andrews, Bristol, Warwick and Newcastle and got their degrees and Cara says, when I was fourteen I realised I *to Pedrouzo* wanted to be a plumber.

Her chin and ears go pointy when she laughs. So I went and did this apprenticeship but it turned out to be more focused on gas stuff.

Now I'm a gas engineer for an agency but what I'd love to do is freelance. I think some people where I live might prefer a lady plumber.

She so much wants to arrive today, we are getting so near now the walk nearly walks itself out, think of that, no more walking!

The markers say 40k, then 37, then 32, then 27... I think I'm going to keep going till I get there tonight, she says.

You can't walk 45k in one day, I tell her.

But think of arriving, she says. The 0,00 sign. I'll just collapse beside the cathedral.

40

I decide that walking alone
brings you closer to God.
Who are you in conversation with, then,
except with

*to Santiago de
Compostela*

in the silvery aerial heights
of the tall trees, in mist

the curved wet leaves
on the ground.

One had less secure roots but lots of berries *Tale of Two*
and blossoms. The other was bare, with a firm *Sister Trees*
foundation. The first asked the other to come and
admire her blossoms: you never visit, she said. The
other replied she was still working on her bark and
root network. The first was coming apart, the bark
splitting and whole clusters of blossoms falling off
and littering the ground. Her roots had become
dislodged, pushed up from their place in the earth
and exposed like a cage, and starting to wither and
dry out in the sun. The wind threatened to carry
her up in a single gust. Please help! she cried. Tie
me to something!

I close my eyes and see the globe in outer space, green and
brown masses suspended in inky blue.
Peer between cotton clouds and spiralling weather
patterns, make out the Iberian peninsula:
    peculiar line
    beetling across the top:

    peregrinos with their packs and roll-mats
    to the end of the known world
    and drop off into sea.

    Now we see from here (in space)
    America and Africa
    grinning from across shores:
    not the end at all.

    Still they score a groove in earth
    – as well towards Makkah, Kumana,
    Gangotri – and do not stop

    to sit in cities, hoarding
    but keep mobile
    and houseless,
    giving in to the river.

*

The last part is concrete, next to the TV towers.
At the hill if you climb to the right place
you can just make out the cathedral: *Monte del Gozo*
pencil-sketch, thumbnail.

                    Gradually

streets. Florists, fruit shops, bakeries
then albergues. Arrows persist.
Someone has dumped their entire rucksack
by a recycling bin, to run for it.

Now the roads funnel
narrowly with chocolate shops and pastry smells,
tourist shops and cafés with colourful
painted signs, then
bagpipes and on the left
one of the doors – locked –

through the arch, round the corner
and into a space like the sky –
a great square filled with rearing horses

and collapsed pilgrims, looking up for something
in the copper-green, bolted doors
and bringing their long outside with them,
the whole way in their bodies

while around them this town, like any town
circulates its business and nonchalance.

Emily wants to feast so we go straight to one of the tapas
bars in the side streets round the cathedral,
   window-glass heaped with croquettes and mariscos.
Emily orders everything: king prawns, scallops, crab and
honey-crusted cod; we drink red, velvety wine and share a
cheesecake-crème brûlée that's cloying, sweet
   but Courtney pushes back her plate: this is not her choice;
all she wants is a bowl of pilgrim pasta, to be in the plain
dark and sleep.
   She stops speaking at the table so we take her back to
the apartment and straightaway both of them enter their
separate bedrooms and shut the door.

Cara sent me a text as we reached Santiago:
Where are you staying?
In an Airbnb with Courtney and Emily.
Is there room for me too?

There's a frilly spare bed beside mine; I ask if Cara can
stay. But Emily wants to keep it to just us three.
   I text back and protect myself. No, sorry.

In the evening we go to the Pilgrim Mass and the
cathedral inside is smaller and gentler than I expected, its
arches round us soft and dim.

A large group of school-girls who walked from Sarría take
turns to hug the apostle, his bust hard and bright with jewels.
   Their white hands materialise on his shoulders

for an instant, then withdraw into the dark.

*   *   *

On the second day I attend a meeting for re-integration,
sitting with tea and biscuits in a circle.

One of the women has just walked the northern way from
Irún: she did the mainstream route some years before.

So what's it like? I'm dying to know. Returning?

When I got home I fell into a deep depression, she says.
I had all of these resolutions and one by one each of them
faded. You think you can hold on to that way of being – like
living each moment, being grateful for the day, and taking
your time, for example. But you just slip back into it.

I roar out the pain of my sister and me.

The Australian priest smiles. The story is a familiar one to
him, he says.

*   *   *

The third day I go to the English Mass.

First we stand and introduce ourselves, and many of the
men stand on behalf of themselves and their wives who don't
get up; we don't see their faces.

Each lights a candle on the altar tray. Most pray for loved
ones at home who are ill or going through a divorce,

and I feel that their world is too small, this chapel
cramped, the man at the front too old and the practice
antiquated, missing the central point.

I almost stand and pray for gender equality in the Church.
But I swallow and ask instead that we might be better
stewards of the Earth.

Thanks. Someone taps me on the shoulder. That was in my

mind too.

Emily and I discuss it later in the flat.

She can't accept a Church like this, that still insists on men running the show.

The thorn lies deep: Christ the Son of Man and God the Father, words difficult to dislodge.

Yes, I say. I know.

I'm on the sofa with Cory and Charlotte, watching Derren Brown on the huge flat-screen.

Who is this megalomaniac? A mind manipulator, is how Cory describes him.

It's a live show where Brown uses techniques of faith healing to conduct miracles on his audience. His pain disappears, her eyesight cured, etc.

but the results are temporary. Of course it's not the work of God, insists Brown – yet strangely enough, the miracle-divine, Biblical spoof-talk is needed to make it work.

Mysterious power of the human will, he says.

You have the choice
of whether to believe
and be healed.

I finished my Camino
                because I had to work

After Santiago I walked
           in three
                    days to the coast

    Fisterra!

    the next day saw me walking to
        the busstation again for a
            connection to Amsterdam.

driving is *overwhelming*
in a whole

new way –

It's fairly mind boggling
I feel a bit

disoriented too.

Yes, it takes time to process

The pace of life in which most of us
function is SO FAST

I'm so mind
boggled in fact I couldn't   remember

all you have experienced

Can't shake the need to walk.

I actually ended up deciding to   head
                    home and be in my own space for a while

I was ready to see my family

with my new   set of eyes Melbourne isn't as bad

as I remember it

                New Orleans helped me remember

        that I love the US as well

        so I'll stay put for now.

the next part of the   journey"...
                              the NEXT Camino). :-)

all this drive
          to be more focussed (hard)
                              on the things I want

Time to knuckle down
              to really work
                          working it all out

                    the next   adventure   to get done

          and   feeling like it's all   possible.

I have so much time   trying to streamline my time

that friendly wish:

        abandon   things

       enjoy the simple

            dance of   everyday

the
comforts of

          Bumblebees in the garden

              my   volunteerjobs in culture and
                                   nature

life is rolling on
for the better

LOVE
change

the
blast

and   magic

As I was trying to find a street sign
for the exhibition,   I found myself

looking to the ground,

standing on

Now i am in Peru but I haven't found

a Camino arrow.

How are you?

What do you love   about being home?

How was your time with your   sister in Leon,
           when the weather   was not "so very good"?

how has been life since then, in your   side? :)

What things are you finding you don't   want to let go of
                                        or adjust back into?

Were there any others you can   remember??

How is your writing   coming?

I've also decided
        i think
    Or maybe
I'm not sure.
    the things that
        I think I've

                        and
                            and I
        THAT

                    and liked that

        Might have been good to
            and possibly
                (thinking

    Like   Maybe   what I

                really want

                that means....

                Thanks

                    11,000+ photos and videos

A few days after coming home, I'm lying on my bed and this image comes to me: a yellowish layer of foam, floating on the water surface.

We spend most of our time there, drifting with the foam. Underneath's an anchor and an iron-hard bed of stone. I have the impression that this stone and anchor, set deep underwater, is reality. The foam, on the other hand, is actually unreal.

The days on Camino were normal; it is the other way around.

*

new leaves have fallen
and we see the backs of
the leaves
like mirrors

furry leaves in the
"wild garden"
by the blue bridge   *River Ouse*

people do sit on benches
under the yellow
crowd of the chestnut tree
looking at water

the round leaves of the
birch, flapping suddenly
like a thousand tambourines

*

I go to Church the first Sunday and cry.

Inside, the stone is ribs and sinew, a growing body or canopy. Everyone is talking and reading the Bible in English, all of the ritual Spanish knocked awake

in messages I can hear.

They walk down the nave with the Gospel, facing the huge, complicated West Window. All of the heads of the people turn like sunflowers.

The priest's a woman with shiny, short black hair. She tells us not to know is OK, to keep asking the questions. I kneel

inside my scallop shell and pray

thank you for bringing me there and here

After the service M. and I go to the shop next door to buy a colourful rag-rug for our bedroom. In the afternoon he shows me a park he's found in the weeks I've been away.

It's quiet and carefully maintained, full of rare garden species, and dazzling with autumn.

At the centre is one red tree, soft as a tongue of flame and deep as a bright pool.

A child makes rings around the tree; like the child, we go to it.

*

I dream I can levitate.

If I focus my mind enough I can rise up, legs crossed in a sitting position, and reach the platform above.

When concentrating fully, I can move my body around in the air like this.

*

A message from Mélany: I am seeking quiet places. In the
tiny medieval church
    folded in its triangle of green
    between Poundland and Tesco
    the volunteer tells me
        calm hangs over here.   *Holy Trinity*
        Except when there's a big school party –
        but it comes back again.

It's cold in the church, and the volunteer stands still
for half a day at a time

*

I dream I am back on Camino but it is winter now.
    I set off uphill and it looks different: there's no-one doing
it in winter; deep bog puddles and frost on the ground.
    I reach a stile and a pony runs at me. Tranquilo. I relax my
muscles, taking the force of the muzzle into my chest.
    The girl whose pony it is comes after it. I walk with her,
back the way we came.
    We stop at an outdoor bar among oak and chestnut trees
and have a strong alcoholic infusion and a good time.
    The girl has become a young man. He holds out a nut like
an acorn, and we look at it together.

*

    There is another square of green, a church-ground, with
only a few old graves, no edifice; silence
    opens out of streets.
        Hold the steady branches   *Bishophill*
        of this Twisted Tree
        as support, a railing

*

One day I walk further than usual, beyond the
Millennium footbridge and slip down to a grassy walkway by
the river, a passage of willow trees.

Where the path ends with fence and hedge, lift up over
bank and follow the crescent edge of meadowland, then
thread the narrow way that leads to the village.

On the left, a house and tower set in its ivy garden, graves
pushed to the sides like paper flaps.

A woman scrambles through the wooden lych-gate with a
man, complaining about an injury; they close it firmly behind
them with a steel loop.

A slinking path by the side of their property leads to a
group of new-build, cream-coloured homes. Between pylons
    peewits whirl and buzz
    in diagonal lines,
    guitar strings.

I am thinking about why certain things happen. For
instance,

> I walked out of one of my exams at university. The
> topics were French poetry, Flaubert and Racine. In
> an old classroom, the invigilator with a silvery bun
> on the back of her head did not smile. I was not able
> to begin the exam and cried into the papers on the
> desk, losing time, crying and losing more time. My
> classmates ignored me, getting their own answers
> down.
>
>   After the first forty minutes I got up and left,
> slumping on the floor outside. I felt liberated.
>
>   I later found out it was relatively common and
> there was a procedure for this. The person on standby

came to rescue me. He was a large, calm man with round glasses, a law professor. For several hours he sat opposite me in the Tutor's office while I continued to cry uncontrollably.

At first he said nothing. Then, when my breathing started to get back to normal, we talked about poetry. He said he hoped the experience would give me an idea for my next poem.

He asked me which paper I enjoyed the most and I said Shakespeare. Had I seen 'Shakespeare in Love'? You should watch it next week, when the exams are over, he said.

It became clear I would actually have to finish the exam later that day. I was taken to a different, more modern building where they held the exams for people allowed extra time or with a disability. I managed to sit and write the exam with forty minutes deducted.

After the tests were over, the next week, I checked my slot for post and there was a slim cardboard parcel next to my name. Inside, the film; no note.

ridges in the pulled-up
asphalt path   *snickelway*

the light: blue
through yellow-glass

*

I dream I am walking again, and the path runs through
a tunnel in an old wall. When I emerge, there is the yellow
arrow, and its familiarity, roughly painted on the ground, is a
deep relief.

Then I am walking down the road towards a village and a
group of hills, softly cut like pieces of felt.

An ox walks beside me, just a few steps ahead to my left.
Its hide is cream-coloured and it's warm, a pink dawn.

*

On Christmas Eve I go out before anyone is up. The
moon's still present, just off full. I am stopped short by a
sheep
    caught up by a fence,
    privately dying. Her leg, lamed,
    scrapes the earth. Eyes closed, mouth firm
    as she endures and suffers.
    I try to give her peace but cannot
    become her or touch her fleece.

We're watching the video of our holiday to Paxos. I am seven, the other two fourteen. Our family is as it was: the five of us. The children on screen don't yet think to make their own lives.

My mother glides through the beautiful Greek heat. I climb with my brother on a spidery tree; my sister suns herself on a pebbly beach.

In the next video we are at home in Curtis Road; it's a few years earlier. My sister lets me help clean out Timmy, her hamster; he scurries and I squeal.

Then she's folded on the blue sofa, her hands busy with some kind of game, pushing strings of elastic out and in and watching children's TV.

She shows the camera her sticker book. Occasionally, if I was lucky, she'd give me one of her most prized shinies.

After the videos the rest of the adults leave to buy nappies and wipes. I stay in the living room and spend the afternoon with my four-year-old niece, making a Lego dragon.

*

January is bare, exposed. They've cleared away the festive tents and huts from the town square and suddenly there's space, lots of sky.

People walk silently across in their coats, on their way to the bank or the market. There are the bleak fingers of tree stubs, manifesting a hush.

*

I dream we have to cross to a different part of the island. We think there should be a ferry but there are just some slender, leaf-shaped boats you have to sail yourself. I get in one and ask my mother to join me but she's scared, then we realise we're meant to have one boat each.

In the new part of the island we don't know where we're supposed to go and everyone's waiting inside the inn.

We are in St. Jean Pied de Port; the people are about to start their Camino. I am responsible for leading the class and they are asking me questions. A girl asks me what she should call God while she walks. I tell her not to worry and that the words will come to her.

One man's already been in St. Jean for fourteen days but finds he can't set out because the town's too beautiful.

*

I cycle past the new-build campus to the swimming pool.

There are bird hides scattered in the shrub around here, my students tell me. They are looking for moments to notice, says Julie.

Like those white birds – I don't
know their name – float up
over the artificial lake   *Heslington East*
in two distinct groups.
The right-hand group settles bodies back down,
on to the water surface.
Then a section of left group joins them, interleaving
in the gaps between the first.
Now each bird has a different neighbour,
and all are woven in.

*

I dream of my sister. She wants a green-and-white striped bag, which used to be mine.

*

I dream that I'm cast as Iago in a production of 'Othello'.
They knew it was unusual, they said, to cast a woman, but
they thought I'd learn the lines and understand it

*

Too hot in February.
The banks are full of litter.
Barbeques, ice cream.

*

I dream that my sister and Mum and Dad and I go
swimming in the pond in front of the house. The neighbour,
David, becomes angry: we are not allowed to swim there.
Upstairs, my sister is shouting at me. You get uglier and
uglier, she says. I almost lash out, then I hug her instead.

*

I am marked with ash: earth, dust, what has been burnt,
muddied, destroyed or disappeared to nothing. They ask us
simply to recall this: we are not made pure, and the journey is
not completed.   *Ash Wednesday*

I cover the page with ashes. What holds through, glows
white? What message is there? Mistakes ring clear: Clare,
Cara.

By the Ouse, the rugby pitch is flooded. The gulls are
using it as their swimming pool; no people today. A flat

expanse of water
   holds its own calm. There is a pair of blackbirds, male-
female, black-
     brown, balanced on the top of the hedge before they dip
     down into leaves. The three
     joyful women

        Rachel   Mélany
            Anne-Lise

     stand with me today
     by the water
     in the mud and sun.

In April I go back. From Santiago I'll walk a final 100km, the four-day way to Finisterre. In the Pilgrim Museum, I try to make sense of the James legends:

> James was in his fishing boat, on the Mountain, in the Garden. When Jesus died, they evangelised: James took 'ends of the earth' literally and chose Finis Terrae, a spot on the far west coast of Hispania and a famous centre for sun worship. His ministry largely failed but the Virgin appeared in a stone barge saying It is finished. You have done well. Back in the Holy Land, he was killed by the authorities.
>
> Two disciples carried his body back to Spain, in another one of those oarless boats of stone. When they reached the shore, a horseman riding along the beach was carried into the foam and driven back on land by the tide, wearing a shirt of scallop shells.
>
> They wanted to bury James in the holiest local plot, perhaps on the grounds of the Sun Altar – but the Roman-Celtic communities, witches and druids there would hear nothing of it. Queen Lupa sent a gang of raving bulls and wolves to snap the disciples' heels, but at the sight of James's
>
> > quiet eyelids, the beasts melted
> > into oxen, and drew the charge
> > to the agreed resting place
> > 100 kilometres inland.

They found a disused sepulchre of green porphyry.
And left him there, until

> after some eight hundred years, a hermit – one
> Pelayo, noticed a glow
> hovering over a certain mound.

Here, history cuts in. About 800 A.D. the Moors were
getting risky, spreading mathematics and civility, right
across Iberia. Alfonso, Asturian king, decided to ramp
up the tomb and make a thing of it, a basilica: sounds
like good business. The town thrived: new-builds
sprouted; lots of lovely shops; leatherwork, jet. When
in another king's dream, the saint arrived on a white
horse

> stamping the infidel,
> that settled it.
> Iago was useful.
> Let them come
> and see with their own eyes.

* * *

At the university, Teresa doesn't believe the route to
Finisterre is part of the real pilgrimage. They call it the
Heathens' Way, she says.
   There's more anticlericalism these days, distrust of the
Church and a turn towards Eastern spiritualities. What do
they want to do, staring at a blank wall?
   Laura comes in here: no, it's capitalism that commodifies,
sucks the heart out.
   And the political dimension, adds Teresa: in Brussels, for

instance, there's a yellow arrow right next to a chunk of the
Berlin Wall. Our European heritage, it's meant to be:
    unity, shared violence. I say what of Santiago Matamoros
    in the cathedral? It's OK,
    they've covered him in flowers, says Teresa.
    Or hidden, I say.

*   *   *

    This is the original entrance, just re-opened after
restoration.
    The statuary's been recoloured pink and gold, lapis lazuli
as it was for the medieval pilgrims, or something like it.
    They'd have had the long view as they drew urgently and
dazzled after many months to this open porch, the buzzing
mouth.
    Today we join a tour, shepherded in groups to the
temperature-controlled zone, to look in our allotted span and
don't touch please, it damages the stone.

Pórtico da Gloria

    Think what it is to arrive
    doorless, into the arms of all of them,
    cherry-cheeked
    and curly-headed –

    the ox hoof on a knee,
    lion's paw – an eagle beak
    fed between fingers –

    and look how their long feet, toes
    curled on their perches are about
    to walk on the air towards you.

Even love the wicked snouts,
winning fangs
and soft-toothed grins
pushing heads
into mouths since the good souls
are carried up in armfuls.

You are here to join the musicians.
That is why we've been singing
all the way. See how he holds
the neck of his viol, side of a harp
or pipe in the pause
before playing, and turns
to mention something to a neighbour.

Come, take a seat,
take bread, and speak
with us, tell us all
that has happened.

*

When I get back to the hotel room there's an envelope on
my bed. I pick it up and something solid shifts around in the
paper.

It's a shell. Brown and weighty, its centre raised like a fist,
with curved, cream-coloured ridges.

There's a note, from Teresa. She bought the shell in
Fisterra with a friend, who died yesterday. She meant to give
it to me at lunch but only remembered after, she writes, in
the cathedral, where she went to pray.

I hang the new shell on my bag, beside the one I've carried
up to now.

The first is thinner and more delicate, with a rose-pink

blush. The red cross inked on its surface is faded from many days of sunlight, knocking to-fro on the move.

Beside it, Teresa's shell swings tough and glossy, darkened and more complex, denser in its patterning.

Take it with you
To Fisterra, she writes.
It comes
From Fisterra.

buddha
on the hillside
for the moment – shifts to
whitened plastic

*from Santiago
de Compostela*

climb above the farm and
the cathedral
   on a white
rained-out sky
    like three minarets
from the horses' field

At every gated house, a guard dog. A few shout, get to
their feet.
   Most stay sitting; many noticing eyes;
also cats.

The last few km, I'm aware it's spring:
the new leaves brushed
apart from branches,
petals on the ground like white
   finger drops glad

2

the rain puts focus on
  the plants. tiny   *from Negreira*
  starshaped clusters

  moss greenly
  oxygenates the road
  margins

  lichen beards
  wrapped around sticks.

    Walking in the fresh, wet but not yet pouring day, my
mind feels transparent.
  Roads unwind like cloth

3

A long straight track.
In sudden bright pauses   *to Santa Marina*
the rain's stopped and you're hearing birds again

4

Over the moor, and to the sea.
Expansive boulders
patched with moss.
A stone cross   *to Cee*
in the middle of a meadow.

First sight of the sea – the curve of it!

Arrive at the beach, thrown into sea
-wind and water mixed with rain;   *Finisterre*
tide green and churning lands
glassy on firm, cream-coloured sand.

On a rectangular trestle laid flat
a hundred shells in colours
grey, pink, lilac, white;
speckled, starred, none alike.

A cup and 'donativo', for Peter.
Peter's nowhere – invisible – sheltered.
His cup is deep with water. I choose a shell,
slide a coin beneath another.

*   *   *

Morning. At the lighthouse there's nothing to see. I climb
the steps to the Visitors' Centre then come back down, walk
round the nose of the headland, my ankle pulsing; the area's all
paved over.

I follow the map up the slope, looking for forests, beaches, magic stones on the other side of the cape. The weather's
unsettled: one moment
too warm and another
the wind cuts my arms.

I turn down a side path, then down an earth track scattered with stones, following signs to the ruins of a hermitage. I pause in the frame of its worn-down walls
where bushes grow. It's quiet as a hollow tree,
but look around and one
adventurer stares down
from his eagle's point
among the walls and leaves.

The paths are a maze, switching back on themselves through forest. I no longer know if the town is this side, or over there, which way to the sea. There are no arrows anymore.

I drop down a slope; then I see the beach, cold scimitar lapped by teal Atlantic. It's lonely, looking out to a nothing in the west, turned away from the pilgrim paths.

But my way twists again and dissolves into scrub and briars. The only way is up; to the left, a sheer muddy chute not meant for feet. I retrace, turning away from the sea. I will just go back to the streets, the albergue.

A wiry woman is power-walking down the track, in shorts and bumbag. Disculpe, I gulp – ¿dónde está – el pueblo? She looks me down, flicks away the map in my hand, then gestures to follow, never slackening her pace as she leaps down the hill, back to precisely the place that I've come from.

Suddenly she stops, draws down her shorts and knickers and spreads her legs to do a wee in the middle of the gravel track. I wait awkwardly.

My guide brings me down a narrow passage I hadn't noticed the first time around, hopping between stones. The path leads between two high walls and into a village.

El pueblo, says the woman, pointing down a lane. ¿Y la playa? She points in the opposite direction, then leaps away.

There are signs: Playa Peligrosa, dangerous beach. A long sequence of boardwalks zigzags over unstable dunes and patches of gorse like poisonous pools. There's a storm shifting in the clouds, turning this way. I sit in the sand for a moment as it stiffens and freshens, rain starting to paint the air. Just a few minutes more.

When I arrived, I reclaimed my bike, slipping the key into the delicate spot to release the plastic-covered band from its loop on the rack. I rode back to college in my soft white dress with red circles, sandals clinging to the pedals in warm evening sunshine. My mind was free and racing; along the street, I counted every church.

I kept my appointment with James. I did not know what I wanted to say. I cried and told him: all this time, in chapel, singing. And I've started to feel, and I think I want to.

He told me he'd noticed, and he wished I could stay longer in the college where he would be preaching. He said that most students would be moving from one kind of institution to another, which would continue to provide them with purpose and structure.

In the weeks that followed, I had no job or study plan. I had a little money left over from my student loan, which was confusing. I decided to travel. I googled
   where to go on a gap year, and
   best journeys to make before you're thirty

I looked up Compostela and somebody's comment popped up:

I first did the Camino in July after graduation. After all those months of sitting in the library, I was ready for a long walk.

I wanted to do it. I hadn't done the training. I asked the internet, When is the right time to go? And someone somewhere had written

   There is no right time to go on pilgrimage.

You don't have to go anywhere
to be on pilgrimage.
When you know, you know: it could be
winter, summer, autumn, spring.

NOTES

p. 84. 'Saint Iago [...] obey the time'. Quotations from *Othello* (c.1603–4) by William Shakespeare, edited by E.A.J. Honigmann. London: Arden, 1997.

p. 97. *'I suspected bad water* [...] *realising it'*. Barbara Haab, "The Way as Inward Journey: An Anthropological Enquiry into the Spirituality of Present-Day Pilgrims to Santiago." Pt. 1, trans. H. Nelson. *Confraternity of St. James Bulletin* 55 (1996): 28–29.

ACKNOWLEDGEMENTS

This project was initially enabled by an Artist's International Development Grant from Arts Council England and the British Council, and later supported by an Author's Foundation Award from the Society of Authors and a residency at the Fondation Jan Michalski: many thanks to these organisations.

Grateful acknowledgement is made to the editors of the following publications in which extracts of this work first appeared: *Wild Court*, *PN Review* and *Bad Lilies*.

Warm thanks to Laura María Lojo Rodríguez and Teresa Sánchez Roura, for welcoming me at the Universidade de Santiago de Compostela in 2019.

Special thanks to James, Gillian, my aunt Gilly, Penny and the Running with Scissors group for comments on the manuscript. To Luke & Sarah, and Nikkola for your encouragement. Thank you, Mike. Thanks to my friends and family for your ongoing support and love.

Thank you to Michael Schmidt, John McAuliffe and the Carcanet team.